i Think: it's Elementary!

Economics and Me

by Mary Hennenfent

"InspirEd" by Kendra Corr and Sharon Coletti

© InspirEd Educators, Inc.   Atlanta, Georgia

** It is the goal of InspirEd Educators to create instructional materials that are interesting, engaging, and challenging. Our student-centered approach incorporates both content and skills, placing particular emphasis on reading, writing, vocabulary development, and critical and creative thinking in the content areas.

Edited by Sharon Coletti and Amy Hellen

Cover graphics by Sharon Coletti and Print1 Direct

Copyright © 2010 by InspirEd Educators, Inc.

ISBN # 978-1-933558082-0

** FOR INDIVIDUAL TEACHER / PARENT USE **

Printed in the United States of America

About InspirEd Educators

InspirEd Educators was founded in 2000 by author Sharon Coletti. Our mission is to provide interesting, student-centered, and thought-provoking instructional materials. To accomplish this, we design lesson plans with standards-based content information presented in a variety of ways and used as the vehicle for developing critical and creative thinking, reading, writing, collaboration, problem-solving, and other necessary and enduring skills. By requiring students to THINK, our lessons ensure FAR greater retention than simple memorization of facts!

Initially our company offered large, comprehensive, multi-disciplinary social studies curricula. Then in 2008 we joined forces with another small company and author, Kendra Corr, and launched our second line of "I Think: Thematic Units," which we've been expanding ever since. These flexible and affordable resources are ideal for individual, small, or large-group instruction. We hope you will find our company's unique approach valuable and that we can serve you again in the near future.

If you are interested in our other offerings, you can find information on our main website at **www.inspirededucators.com**.

InspirEd Educators materials provide engaging lesson plans that vary daily and include:

- Lesson-specific Springboards (warm-ups)
- Writing activities
- Critical and creative thinking
- Problem-solving
- Test-taking skill development
- Primary source analyses (DBQ's)
- Multiple perspectives
- Graphic analyses
- Fascinating readings
- Simulations
- Story-telling
- Practical use of technology
- Debates
- Plays
- Research
- Graphic organizers
- AND SO MUCH MORE!!!!!

Thank you for choosing our units,
Sharon Coletti, President
InspirEd Educators

Tips for Teaching with this InspirEd Unit

- Before beginning the unit, take time to look through the Objectives and lessons. This will give you a chance to think about what you want to emphasize and decide upon any modifications, connections, or extensions you'd like to include.

- Arrange for your student(s) to have books available or to check them out. A suggested reading list is included, but any books of interest related to the unit subject are fine. We do strongly suggest the reading link to enhance this study! Activities are included that refer to the book(s) being read, and students should be encouraged to discuss any connections throughout.

- Give your student(s) a copy of the Objective page at the beginning of unit study. The Objectives serve as an outline of the content to be covered and provide a means to review information. Have the student(s) define the vocabulary terms as they progress through the lessons and thoroughly answer the essential questions. You can review their responses as you go along or wait and check everything as a test review. It is important that your student(s) have some opportunity to receive feedback on their Objective answers, since assessments provided at the end of the unit are based on these.

- Read through each lesson's materials before beginning. This will help you better understand lesson concepts; decide when and how to present the vocabulary and prepare the handouts (or transparencies) you will need.

- "Terms to know" can be introduced at the beginning of lessons or reviewed at the end, unless specified otherwise. (In a few instances the intent is for students to discover the meanings of the terms.)

- Our materials are intended to prompt discussion. Often students' answers may vary, but it's important that they be able to substantiate their opinions and ideas with facts. Let the discussion flow!

- Note that differentiated assessments are provided at the end of the unit. Feel free to use any of these as appropriate; cut-and-paste to revise, or create your own tests as desired.

- For additional information and research sites refer to the Resource Section in the back of the unit.

- InspirEd Educators units are all about thinking and creativity, so allow yourself the freedom to adapt the materials as you see fit. Our goal is to provide a springboard for you to jump from in your teaching and your student(s)' learning.

- ENJOY! We at InspirEd Educators truly believe that teaching and learning should be enjoyable, so we do our best to make our lessons interesting and varied. We want you and your student(s) to love learning!

TABLE OF CONTENTS

Some Suggested Reading

NOTE: Depending upon ability, have your student(s) read one or more of the following titles (or others as available) on the topic of Economics to accompany this unit study.

Aaseng, Nathan, <u>From Rags to Riches: People Who Started Businesses from Scratch</u>, Lerner Publications Co., 1990.

Bouani, Jennifer, <u>Tyler and His Solve-A- Matic Machine</u>, Bouje Publishing 2006.

Bouani, Jennifer, <u>Tyler Passes the Golden Key</u>, Bouje Publishing, 2008.

Catran, Ken, <u>Fries</u>, Lothian Books, 2002.

Clements, Andrew, <u>Lunch Money</u>, Atheneum, 2007.

Curtis, Christopher Paul, <u>Mr. Chickee's Funny Money</u>, Yearling, 2007.

Dahl, Roald, <u>Charlie and the Chocolate Factory</u>, Puffin Books, 2007.

Danzinger, Paula, <u>Not for a Billion Gazillion Dollars</u>, Putnam Juvenile, 1998.

Davies, Jacqueline<u>, The Lemonade Wars</u>, Sandpiper, 2009.

Epstein, Rachel, <u>Estee Lauder: Beauty Business Success</u>, Franklin Watts, 2000.

Haskins, Jim, <u>African American Entrepreneurs</u>, Wiley, 1998.

Karnes, Frances, <u>A. Girls and Young Women Entrepreneurs; True Stories About Starting and Running a Business Plus How You Can Do It Yourself</u>, Free Spirit Publishing, 1997.

Laughllin, Rosemary, <u>John D. Rockefeller: Oil Baron and Philanthropist</u>, Morgan Reynolds Publishing, 2004.

Lesinski, Jeanne, M. <u>Bill Gates</u>, First Avenue Editions, 2006.

Moore, Billy, <u>Cracker's Mule</u>, Junebug Books, 2003

New Moon Books Girls Editorial Board, <u>New Moon: Money</u>, Crown Books for Young Readers, 2000.

Paulsen, Gary, <u>Lawn Boy</u>, Wendy Lamb Books, 2007.

Welles, Lee, <u>Gaia Girls Enter the Earth</u>, Daisyworld Press, 2007.

Weston, Robin, <u>Oprah Winfrey: I Don't Believe in Failure</u>, Enslow Publishers, 2005.

ECONOMICS OBJECTIVES

Define and be able to use these terms:

- scarcity
- resources
- renewable
- economics
- goods
- services
- consumer
- consume
- profit
- import
- export
- interest
- deposit
- withdrawal
- balance
- opportunity cost
- budget
- expense
- factors of production
- labor
- capital
- entrepreneur
- advertise
- competition
- barter
- supply
- demand
- currency
- money
- industry
- monopoly
- production
- assembly line
- specialization
- technology
- taxes
- citizen
- interdependence
- embargo
- trade balance
- synthetic
- environment
- debate

Fully answer the following questions:

1. Explain how various types of resources are used to meet needs and wants.
2. Describe the four sectors of an economy.
3. Explain how spending and saving affects the economy.
4. Describe the factors of production.
5. Explain how supply and demand works between consumers and sellers.
6. Explain how competition and specialization affects the business sector.
7. Describe the role of the government sector in an economy.
8. Describe the various types of economies.
9. Explain interdependence and problems that can result.
10. Describe the push-pull that takes place between the needs of an economy and the environment.

ECONOMICS OBJECTIVES ANSWERS AND EXPLANATIONS

Define and be able to use these terms:
Definitions for terms are provided in the lessons in which they are introduced.

Fully answer the following questions:

1. *Resources include everything used to meet the wants and needs of people. They can either be human (workers and things made by workers) or natural (taken from nature). These resources are used to make goods (things that can be bought) or services (work done for pay) that consumers want and need.*

2. *An economy includes the household sector (consumers), the business sector (that produces goods and services), the government (makes laws to ensure the economy runs smoothly and provides services), and the foreign sector (imports brought into a country and exports sold to other nations).*

3. *When consumers decide whether or not to spend their money on goods and services, they should consider the opportunity costs, what they are giving up. Although saving is important, it is also necessary for consumers to buy goods and services to keep sellers in business. Consumers' budgets must also be considered in spending decisions.*

4. *The factors of production include everything needed to make goods and provide services. This includes resources (man-made and from nature), labor (workers) and capital (money, buildings, and machines needed). Entrepreneurs, those who take risks to open and run businesses, are also needed for the business sector to function properly. They are sometimes called the fifth factor of production.*

5. *Goods are bought and sold based on the amount of product available (the supply) and what is wanted or needed (the demand). When goods are in high demand, or low supply, prices tend to be higher because people are willing to spend more. On the other hand, when goods are in low demand or high supply, prices will tend to be lower since there is plenty to go around.*

6. *There are many ways for sellers to make profits. They must stand out from others in their industry at attract more consumers. They do this by offering deals, advertising, etc. To increase profits, businesses may specialize (do one thing well) or engage in mass production (to make goods faster and cheaper).*

7. *The government sector not only makes rules to govern how the economy works, but also provides various good and services for consumers such as parks, police and fire departments, and other services. These services are paid for with tax dollars from consumers and businesses.*

8. *There are three types of economies: market in which people are free to own businesses and buy and sell what they want; command in which a government makes these decisions); and mixed, a combination of citizen and government decision-making.*

9. *Since countries produce different things, they come to rely on one another for certain goods and services to import and export. However efforts should be made to balance imports and exports as much as possible.*

10. *Conflicts can arise when concerns about the environment clash with the needs of the economy. In fact many economic decisions must take into account both community development and jobs and environmental protection.*

What's It All About?

Springboard:
Students should complete the "Wants & Needs" handout.
*(Lists and answers may vary, but should reflect the understanding
that wants are optional, while needs MUST be met to survive.)*

Objective: The student will be able to explain how people's wants and needs are met with natural and human resources.

Materials:
Wants & Needs (Springboard handout)
Clued In Cards (cut up cards)
Which is Which (handout)

Terms to know:
scarcity - not enough of something
resources - used to meet wants and needs
renewable - something that is not likely to run out
economics - how resources are used to meet people's wants and needs

Procedure:

· During discussion of the last Springboard question, introduce the term "scarcity" and have the student(s) identify items on their lists that are scarce can explain why. Explain that *resources (review term) are used to meet our needs and wants*.

· **For group instruction** have students work in pairs, each with a set of "Clued In Cards" and a "Which is Which" handout. **For individualized instruction** the teacher/parent should play the game with the student.

· Explain that *resources come in two main types: human resources include workers and all the things made by workers, and natural resources are taken directly from nature*. Then explain the rules as follows:

   1. The students should divide the cards into two piles, face down, without looking at them. Each pair should take turns looking at a card and giving his/her partner clues to describe the item (one clue at a time, up to three clues total). A player that draws a blank card must fill in the blank and then provide clues.

   2. When a player guesses an item correctly, the pair should place the card under the correct heading on the "Which is Which?" handout.

   3. If a player cannot guess after three clues, the card should return to the bottom of the pile. If, after a card comes up a second time and is not guessed correctly, the card should be added to the handout regardless.

· Have the student(s) share their groupings and "added" items. Introduce the term "renewable" and have the student(s) tell which things on their charts are renewable. *(Natural resources: tree, rock, fish, water, oil, sun, wind, soil, plus any added. All others are human or human-made. Rock, sun, wind, and soil are examples of renewable resources.)*

· Explain (and write as appropriate) that *economics is the way we use our scarce resources to meet people's needs and wants*.

WANTS & NEEDS

DIRECTIONS: Fill up as many spaces as you can for each category. Then answer the questions at the bottom of the page.

I WANT...   I NEED...

_____ _____   _____ _____
_____ _____   _____ _____
_____ _____   _____ _____
_____ _____   _____ _____
_____ _____   _____ _____
_____ _____   _____ _____
_____ _____   _____ _____
_____ _____   _____ _____
_____ _____   _____ _____
_____ _____   _____ _____

What is the difference between **wants** and **needs**? _____
_____
_____

How do we get what we want and need? _____
_____
_____

Can we have **everything** we want and need? Why or why not? _____
_____
_____

Clued In Cards

Tree	Hammer	Tractor
Truck	Chef	Rock
Salesman	Fish	Computer
Doctor	Water	Oil
Teacher	Sun	Factory
Wind	Painter	Electricity
Soil	Corn	Manager
Shovel	Pilot	Pencil

WHICH is WHICH

Natural Resources	Human Resources

I Got the Goods (and Services)

Objective: The student will be able to describe how consumers buy and use goods and services.

Materials: Goods and Services Cards (Springboard cut-out set per student - save for next lesson)
Goods and Services (handout)
Compare + Contrast (handout)

Terms to know: **goods** - items that can be bought or sold
services - work done for someone else
consumer - someone who buys goods and services

Procedure:

- While reviewing the Springboard, have the student(s) try to divide their answers into two groups based on what the items have in common.

- Have them share their groupings. *(Answers may vary, but if it isn't noted, point out that <u>one way to divide the items is into "goods" and "services."</u> Introduce the terms.)*

- Distribute the "Goods and Services" handout, and introduce the term "consumer." Explain that <u>in this lesson the student(s) will act as consumers of goods and services.</u>

- **For group instruction** divide students into threes and have group members each choose one the following roles: Mom or Dad, Grocery Store Owner, and Town Mayor. **For individualized instruction** omit one role; the parent/teacher and student should play the remaining two.

- Each player (in his/her role) should brainstorm a list of goods and services that the person would need.

- Then have the groups compare and contrast the lists they made, using the triple Venn diagram provided on the "Compare + Contrast" handout. **For individualized instruction** the student should fill in two of the three circles or create his/her own Venn diagram.

- Have student(s) share and compare their diagrams by posting them around the room and having student(s) "gallery walk" the room to examine others' work.

GOODS & SERVICES cards

Where can you get gas for your car?	Where can you buy food?	Where can you buy new clothes?
Where can you get your clothes cleaned?	Where can you safely put a paycheck?	Where do you go to rent a movie?
Where can you see the newest movie?	Where can you buy stamps to mail a letter?	Where can you get a haircut?
Where can you get a hamburger?	Where can you buy a car?	Where can you go to get a cavity filled?
Where can you buy school supplies?	Where can you get a new pet?	Where can you stay when you go to another city?
Where can you get a book?	Where can you report a crime?	Where can you buy a friend's birthday present?
Where can you learn how to speak Spanish?	Where can you go to see a live band?	Where can you get music downloads?
Where can you recycle newspapers?	Where can you get a new computer?	Where can you take singing lessons?

Goods and Services

Role: _____

Goods You'll Need	Services You'll Need

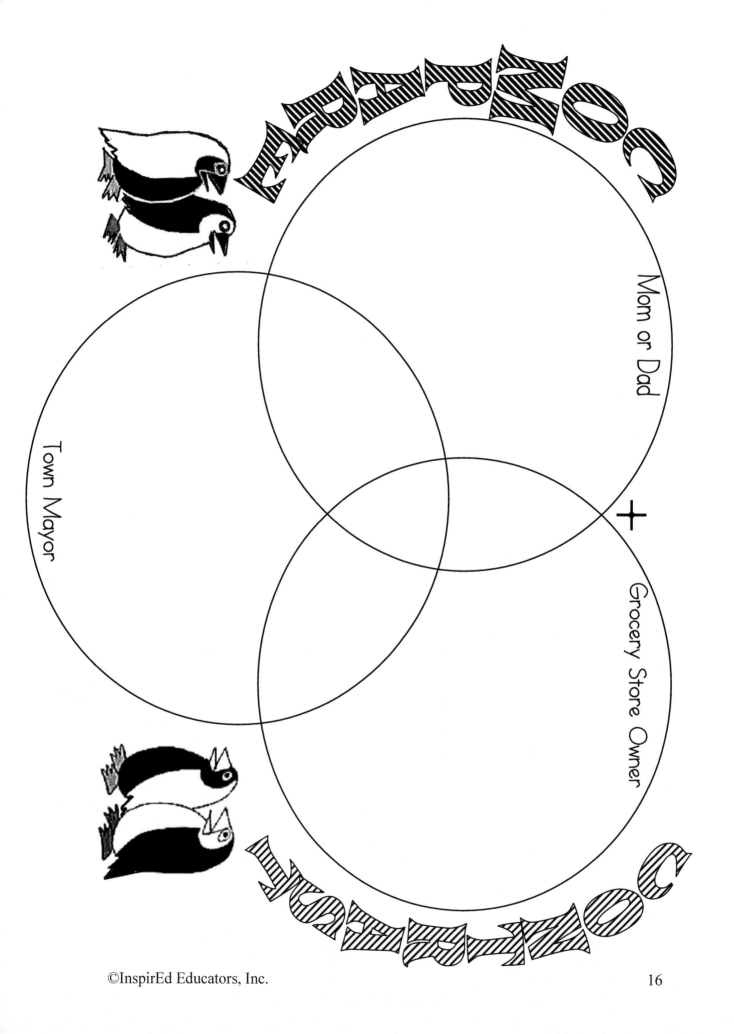

COMPARE

Town Mayor

Mom or Dad

+

Grocery Store Owner

CONTRAST

Putting It All Together

> **Springboard:**
>   Students should read "What's An Economy?" and answer the questions.

Objective: The student will be able to describe the four sectors of an economy.

Materials:
What's an Economy? (Springboard handout)
Goods and Services Cards (from previous lesson)
Building a Community (handout)
butcher or other large-sized paper
markers or crayons
construction paper (optional – See NOTE)
glue or tape (optional – See NOTE)

Terms to know:
consume - buy goods and services
profit - money made from business
import - good brought in; bringing goods in from other countries
export - good sent out; the sending of goods to other countries for sale

Procedure:
· After reviewing the Springboard, explain that _in this lesson the student(s) will create a model community that includes the four sectors of an economy_.
· Have the student(s) take out their Goods and Services cards from the previous lesson and distribute the "Building a Community" handout. Review the directions, but don't have the student(s) answer the analysis questions yet.
· Allow time to complete the community model. **For group instruction** the students should work groups of four to six. **For individualized instruction** the student can work with the parent/teacher. (**NOTE:** If desired, students could draw all elements of their communities instead of making the 3-D model explained on the handout.)
· Once they have completed their models, the student(s) should THEN complete the analysis.
· Have them share/compare models and analyses. _Explain that in the following lessons, the student(s) will examine each sector in more detail_.

WHAT'S AN ECONOMY?

An economy is the way people use resources to meet their wants and needs. People can make, trade, buy, sell, and use goods and services. But people are not the only ones to make, trade, buy, sell, and use. In fact there are four **sectors** of an economy.

The household sector includes all who consume. In other words, they buy and use goods and services. The business sector is next. It makes the goods and services using natural and human resources. The goal of a business is to make a profit on the goods or services it sells. The business sector tries to offer goods and services people need and want. Products are made and services are offered for a price that allows the business to make money.

The third economic sector is the government. The government's job is to make laws and rules to help the economy run smoothly. Laws and rules can control how goods and services are made, traded, bought, sold, and used. The government can make laws to control how goods are made or to make sure consumers aren't cheated. It can limit who can buy or use certain products. The fourth sector of an economy is the foreign sector. This includes imports brought into a country and exports sold to other countries.

The four sectors are all important to keep an economy working. And they all relate to each other in many ways. If the household sector doesn't buy things, the business sector cannot make profits. And fewer goods will be imported. If the government makes too many rules, it can be hard for countries to sell us their exports. If a country doesn't buy imports, other countries may not want to buy its products. There are many other ways these four sectors connect. All four must work together for an economy to be strong.

The word "sectors" in the reading **MOST NEARLY** means
    A. laws.   B. consumers.   C. parts.   D. ways.

Which **BEST** shows a business making a good profit?
    A. A clothing store buys blue jeans for $25 to sell for $50.
    B. A gas station charges more than all the others in the city.
    C. A local flower shop always buys much more than it sells.
    D. A restaurant serves terrible food and treats people badly.

One way the government sector can limit consumers is a
    A. factory cannot pollute the water it uses.
    B. product from China says where it is made.
    C. teen must be at least 16 to drive in the U.S.
    D. drug company must warn about side effects.

Explain what you think a "good economy" is like? _____

_____

_____

_____

An economy is the way people use resources to meet their wants and needs. People can make, trade, buy, sell, and use goods and services. But people are not the only ones to make, trade, buy, sell, and use. In fact there are four **sectors** of an economy.

The household sector includes all who consume. In other words, they buy and use goods and services. The business sector is next. It makes the goods and services using natural and human resources. The goal of a business is to make a profit on the goods or services it sells. The business sector tries to offer goods and services people need and want. Products are made and services are offered for a price that allows the business to make money.

The third economic sector is the government. The government's job is to make laws and rules to help the economy run smoothly. Laws and rules can control how goods and services are made, traded, bought, sold, and used. The government can make laws to control how goods are made or to make sure consumers aren't cheated. It can limit who can buy or use certain products. The fourth sector of an economy is the foreign sector. This includes imports brought into a country and exports sold to other countries.

The four sectors are all important to keep an economy working. And they all relate to each other in many ways. If the household sector doesn't buy things, the business sector cannot make profits. And fewer goods will be imported. If the government makes too many rules, it can be hard for countries to sell us their exports. If a country doesn't buy imports, other countries may not want to buy its products. There are many other ways these four sectors connect. All four must work together for an economy to be strong.

The word "sectors" in the reading **MOST NEARLY** means
    A. laws.   B. consumers.   C. parts. *   D. ways.
    (If each word is substituted for "sectors," Choice C makes the most sense.)

Which **BEST** shows a business making a good profit?
    A. A clothing store buys blue jeans for $25 to sell for $50. *
    B. A gas station charges more than all the others in the city.
    C. A local flower shop always buys much more than it sells.
    D. A restaurant serves terrible food and treats people badly.
    (Choices B and D would likely have few people buying from them, and C has so much waste it's hard to make money. A is the best example of making a profit.)

One way the government sector can limit consumers is a
    A. factory cannot pollute the water it uses.
    B. product from China says where it is made.
    C. teen must be at least 16 to drive in the U.S. *
    D. drug company must warn about side effects.

(Choices A and D limit producers and Choice B limits a country. Only C limits a CONSUMER.)

Explain what you think a "good economy" is like? *The last paragraph points out several interactions. In a "good" or "strong" economy all sectors work and work well together. People buy what businesses sell, following the laws and rules established by the government. Goods from the business sector are exported to other countries, and other countries' goods are sold and bought.*

BUILDING A  COMMUNITY

DIRECTIONS: Use the supplies on hand to create a community model. Include the buildings and other structures described on the goods and services cards. Add homes, roads, and a river. Label or color-code to show the following in some way:

- goods
- services
- household sector
- business sector
- government sector
- foreign sector

Be sure to include a key if needed. Keep in mind, also, that some things may fit more than one category!

Then answer these questions about your community:

1. Does your community have more goods or services? Do you think this is the case in most places? Why or why not?

2. What goods and services do you think are missing in this community? What else do you think needs to be there? Why?

3. Explain at least one way that two or more of the economic sectors work together in your community.

4. Explain one way your community uses its resources to meet its needs and wants.

To Spend or Not to Spend

Springboard:

Students should read "A Tale of Three Friends" and answer the questions.

Objective: The student will be able to explain the importance of saving money.

Materials:
A Tale of Three Friends (Springboard handout)
Balancing the Books Game (handout)
Balancing the Books Cards (2 pages; cut-out and shuffled)
Putting in Your 2¢ (2-page handout)

Terms to know:
interest - money earned from the bank for deposits
deposit - money put into a bank account
withdrawal - money taken out of a bank account
balance - amount of money in an account
opportunity cost - whatever is given up in a choice to spend and/or save

Procedure:

- After reviewing the Springboard, explain that _people in the household sector often have to make decisions about whether to spend their money on goods and services, or to save it for something else._ Go on to explain that _in this lesson the student(s) will learn how spending and saving can affect the economy._

- Distribute a "Balancing the Books Game" handout to each student and a set of game cards to each pair or group. **For group instruction** have the students form groups of 3-4. **For individualized instruction the** parent/teacher should play with the student. Review the directions and explain that _this game demonstrates how money can be earned and spent._ Then have the student(s) play until only one player is left with money. If time is a factor, the player with the most money at the end of the allotted time wins.

- Distribute the "Putting in Your 2¢" handout and introduce the term "opportunity cost." Then have the student(s) complete the debriefing analysis on their own or in their playing groups.

- Have them share / compare their ideas and discuss. _(Answers will vary for most questions but the following points should be emphasized:_
  o _Saving money is important, because money is not always easy to come by._
  o _Saving is often necessary for big and important purchases such as homes, cars, college, etc._
  o _The bank is the safest place to keep your savings, and it earns interest._
  o _Though saving is a good habit to learn, wise spending is also important._
  o _It is wise to consider opportunity costs when making decisions about spending and saving._

A Tale of Three Friends

Jake, Mike and Tony are close friends. But, the three are always trying to outdo each other. One way they compete is with video games. Each time a new game comes out all three want to be the first to buy it. They all want to practice before playing the game together. The newest game they want costs $29.00.

The three boys each get $20.00 a month for doing chores. But the friends all have very different savings habits! Jake always carries his money around with him in case he sees something he wants to buy. Mike puts his money in a jar in his room so he won't be tempted to spend it. Tony puts half of his money in a savings account every month at the local bank. The bank pays him 2% interest each month. So he earns an additional 20 cents on his money every month.

The three boys also have very different spending habits. Jake figures his money is easy to earn, so he spends half of it each month. Mike loves going to the movies. So he dips into his jar and spends $12.00 each month on movie tickets. Tony never fails to stick to his savings plan, but spends the other half of his monthly money on things he wants or needs.

Based on their habits, which boy will be able to save up enough to buy the video game first? Explain your answer._____

_____

_____

_____

How long will it take that boy to save the money for the video game? What about the other two boys? _____

_____

_____

Which boy do you think has the best money habits? Why?_____

_____

_____

_____

Which boy do you think has the worst money habits? Why? _____

_____

_____

_____

_____

A Tale of Three Friends
Suggestions for Answers

Jake, Mike and Tony are close friends. But, the three are always trying to outdo each other. One way they compete is with video games. Each time a new game comes out all three want to be the first to buy it. They all want to practice before playing the game together. The newest game they want costs $29.00.

The three boys each get $20.00 a month for doing chores. But the friends all have very different savings habits! Jake always carries his money around with him in case he sees something he wants to buy. Mike puts his money in a jar in his room so he won't be tempted to spend it. Tony puts half of his money in a savings account every month at the local bank. The bank pays him 2% interest each month. So he earns an additional 20 cents on his money every month.

The three boys also have very different spending habits. Jake figures his money is easy to earn, so he spends half of it each month. Mike loves going to the movies. So he dips into his jar and spends $12.00 each month on movie tickets. Tony never fails to stick to his savings plan, but spends the other half of his monthly money on things he wants or needs.

Based on their habits, which boy will be able to save up enough to buy the video game first? Explain your answer. *Jake saves $5 per month and spends $15 on whatever he wants. Mike saves $8 per month and spends $12 on movies. Tony saves $10.20 per month, since he puts $10 in the bank and earns $.20 per month in interest. Therefore Tony will be able to buy the game first because he saves the most every month.*

How long will it take that boy to save the money for the video game? What about the other two boys? *It will take Tony three months to save for the game ($10.20 x 3 months = $30.60). It will take Jake six months to save for the game ($5 x 6 months = $30.00). It will take Mike four months to save for the game ($8 x 4 = $32.00).*

Which boy do you think has the best money habits? Why? *Answers may vary but should be explained. Students may note that using a bank is a smart move because it keeps your money safe and earns interest.*

Which boy do you think has the worst money habits? Why?
Students will probably criticize Jake carrying his money around because it could get lost or stolen. Opinions on the boys' approaches to saving money may vary.

Balancing the Books Game

DIRECTIONS: Players begin with $100 in their bank account. On each turn a player picks a card and enters the value as a deposit (+) or a withdrawal (-) into the account and figures the new balance. Every third turn, 5% interest (balance x .05 or 5%) should be added to the balance as a deposit. Players remain in the game until their balance falls to $0 or below. The winner is the last player standing or with the most money when play ends.

Deposit (+)	Withdrawal (-)	Balance
		$100

Balancing the Books Game Cards

Earn allowance of $10.00	Earn allowance of $10.00	Earn allowance of $10.00
Earn allowance of $10.00	Earn allowance of $10.00	Earn allowance of $10.00
Earn $20.00 babysitting	Earn $20.00 babysitting	Earn $20.00 babysitting
Earn $20.00 mowing lawns	Earn $20.00 mowing lawns	Earn $20.00 mowing lawns
Earn $15.00 shoveling snow	Earn $15.00 shoveling snow	Earn $15.00 shoveling snow
Earn $20.00 pet-sitting	Earn $20.00 pet-sitting	Earn $20.00 pet-sitting
Earn $10.00 for extra chores	Earn $10.00 for extra chores	Earn $10.00 for extra chores
Get $50.00 for your birthday	Get $50.00 for your birthday	Get $50.00 for your birthday
Get $20 from visiting relatives	Get $20 from visiting relatives	Get $20 from visiting relatives
Get $10.00 for straight A's	Get $10.00 for straight A's	Get $10.00 for straight A's
Earn $10.00 helping neighbors	Earn $10.00 helping neighbors	Earn $10.00 helping neighbors
Get $20 from visiting relatives	Get $20 from visiting relatives	Get $20 from visiting relatives

Spend $10 on a movie	Spend $10 on a movie	Spend $10 on a movie
Spend $15 on bowling	Spend $15 on bowling	Spend $15 on bowling
Spend $25 on a video game	Spend $25 on a video game	Spend $25 on a video game
Spend $20 on a gift	Spend $20 on a gift	Spend $20 on a gift
Spend $10 on books	Spend $10 on books	Spend $10 on books
Spend $20 on clothes	Spend $20 on clothes	Spend $20 on clothes
Spend $5 on fast food	Spend $5 on fast food	Spend $5 on fast food
Spend $15 on a new CD	Spend $15 on a new CD	Spend $15 on a new CD
Spend $20 at the mall	Spend $20 at the mall	Spend $20 at the mall
Spend $15 at the arcade	Spend $15 at the arcade	Spend $15 at the arcade
Lose $15 broke Mom's vase!	Lose $15 broke Mom's vase!	Lose $15 broke Mom's vase!
Lose $10 out of your pocket!	Lose $10 out of your pocket!	Lose $10 out of your pocket!

Putting In Your 2¢

1. What are the some ways you can get and lose money?_____

_____

_____

_____

_____

2. If you have a choice, what are some things you would **NOT** spend money on? Why?_____

_____

_____

_____

3. What are some things you might save for? _____

_____

_____

4. Whether you spend or save, there is always an "opportunity cost" involved. It is what you give up by making the decision you do. Name at least **3** examples of opportunity costs of spending and saving in the game. _____

_____

_____

_____

_____

5. Explain what is **GOOD** about saving money. _____

_____

_____

_____

6. Explain the negatives of saving money in terms of opportunity cost.

_____

_____

_____

_____

7. Explain what is **GOOD** about spending money. _____

_____

_____

_____

8. Explain the negatives of spending money in terms of opportunity cost.

_____

_____

_____

9. What questions should you ask yourself before spending or saving money? _____

_____

_____

10. Briefly explain what you think is a good plan for spending and saving.

_____

_____

_____

_____

11. What did you learn about spending and saving from playing this game? _____

_____

_____

12. Do you think you will change your spending or saving habits based on this lesson? Explain. _____

_____

_____

_____

_____

Tightening the Belt

Springboard:
Students should complete the "Is This Really Necessary?" handout.
(Answers will vary but should be explained.)

Objective: The student will be able to explain how keeping to a budget can impact our choices.

Materials:
Is This Really Necessary? (Springboard handout)
Budget Cards (cut-outs - 1 per group of 3-4 *)
Planning a Party (handout)

Terms to know:
budget - a plan for spending
expense - cost of goods or services

Procedure:

- After reviewing the Springboard, explain that *budgets are a good way for consumers to keep track of their spending. They can also help us identify what we really need, versus what we may want*. Go on to explain that *in this lesson the student(s) will plan a party on a budget*.

- **For group instruction** distribute one of the "Budget Cards" to each group of three or four students. ***For individualized instruction** the student should complete the activity with parent / teacher help, as needed.

- Then distribute the "Planning a Party" handout. The student(s) should use the Internet to "shop" for the items needed and keep track of their purchases for their party on the form. Depending upon your student(s) ability level, it may be helpful to recommend specific websites such as discount department stores or party stores: **www.birthdayexpress.com** and **www.birthdaydirect.com**.

- Have the groups share their budgets, responses, and the challenges they faced shopping on budget. Ask them to explain how having a budget impacted their choices. (*They couldn't buy whatever they wanted, they had to make some sacrifices- opportunity costs, they had to shop around for better prices, etc.*)

is this really necessary?

DIRECTIONS: Study the monthly budget below and tell if each item is a need or a want.

Item	Expense	Need or Want
house payment	$1,100	
car payment	$250	
electricity	$50	
water	$23	
cable TV	$65	
telephone	$45	
Internet	$40	
groceries	$400	
medical insurance	$500	
entertainment	$200	
clothing	$100	
cell phone	$50	
TOTAL:	$2823.00	

If this person earned $2200.00 per month, what would you suggest be cut from this budget? Why? _____

_____

_____

_____

In what ways can a budget (like this one) be helpful? _____

_____

_____

_____

Budget Cards

Budget: $50	Number of Guests: 5	Occasion: Birthday Party
Budget: $50	Number of Guests: 10	Occasion: Birthday Party
Budget: $100	Number of Guests: 8	Occasion: Birthday Party
Budget: $100	Number of Guests: 15	Occasion: Birthday Party
Budget: $100	Number of Guests: 20	Occasion: Birthday Party
Budget: $200	Number of Guests: 10	Occasion: Birthday Party
Budget: $200	Number of Guests: 16	Occasion: Birthday Party
Budget: $200	Number of Guests: 20	Occasion: Birthday Party
Budget: $300	Number of Guests: 10	Occasion: Birthday Party
Budget: $300	Number of Guests: 20	Occasion: Birthday Party

DIRECTIONS: Below is a list of things that could be bought for your party. (Use the blank spaces for anything else you think of. Do research to find out how much each item will cost. Keep in mind the number of guests as you shop. You'll need to "buy" enough for everyone.

Shopping List	Store / website	Cost per Item	Total Cost
Invitations			
Plates			
Cups			
Napkins			
Decorations			
Forks			
Games			
Prizes			
Drinks			
Cake			
Goodie bags			

How did you "cut corners" to stay within your budget? _____

_____

_____

How did opportunity costs impact your decisions in spending money? _____

_____

_____

_____

How did having to stick to a budget impact your choices? _____

_____

_____

_____

_____

What a Production!

Springboard:

Students should put the steps of "Making Crayons" in the proper order from 1 to 10.

(*From top to bottom: 7, 9, 3, 6, 5, 1, 4, 10, 8, 2*)

Objective: The student will describe factors involved in production of goods and services.

Materials:
Making Crayons (Springboard handout)
Open for Business (handout)
Factors of Production (handout)

Terms to know:
factors of production - all that is needed to provide goods and services
labor - workers
capital - money, buildings, machines needed to produce

Procedure:

• After reviewing the Springboard, explain that *everything involved in making crayons are called the factors of production* (*review term*). Go on to explain that *in this lesson the student(s) will more closely examine the business sector and how it uses the factors of production to start new businesses.*

• Distribute the "Open for Business" brainstorming form, and review the directions, encouraging the student(s) to *think of **EVERY DETAIL** they can!* Ideally they should work in pairs or small groups to think of a business of interest and fill in the blanks with whatever would be needed to open and run that business.

• Have them share their lists, adding things others suggest that they forgot.

• Then distribute "Factors of Production." The student(s) should "sort" their lists into the three categories and answer the analysis questions. (*Answers could include:*

1. *As long as the answer is justified, any of the factors are acceptable. During discussion of this question, point out that capital usually involves more money than the other two. Buildings and equipment are expensive, and cash is needed to pay workers and buy resources.*
2. *Answers may vary: banks; loans from friends, families, or others; etc.*
3. *Answers will vary but entrepreneurship is addressed in the next lesson.*
4. *Often a new business will NOT show a profit right away. Business owners usually need enough money to START the business AND live for a while.*

• **EXTENSION #1:** Student(s) can view the online video "How Crayons Are Made" @ http://pbskids.org/rogers/video_crayons.html.

• **EXTENSION #2:** Directions and great ideas for crayon recycling can be found @ http://www.epinions.com/content_4914847876.

MAKING CRAYONS

DIRECTIONS: Number the steps to making a crayon in the order they **SHOULD** be done – from 1 to 10.

Workers stack the crayons into a machine to wrap the labels on them.	
Crayon boxes are then packed by workers into large boxes.	
Workers add powder to the wax to make it harden.	
Workers remove the crayons from the molds.	
Workers pour the colored wax into molds.	
Trains bring wax and other supplies to the crayon factory.	
Workers then add color to the hardened wax.	
Trucks take the crayons to stores where they are sold.	
Workers load the crayons into another machine that puts one of each color into a box.	
The wax is poured into a big kettle.	

OPEN FOR BUSINESS

Kind of business you are "opening" _____

DIRECTIONS: List **EVERYTHING** you can think of that you will need to open and run your business. Can you fill in **ALL** the blanks?!

_____	_____	_____
_____	_____	_____
_____	_____	_____
_____	_____	_____
_____	_____	_____
_____	_____	_____
_____	_____	_____
_____	_____	_____
_____	_____	_____
_____	_____	_____
_____	_____	_____
_____	_____	_____
_____	_____	_____
_____	_____	_____
_____	_____	_____
_____	_____	_____
_____	_____	_____
_____	_____	_____
_____	_____	_____
_____	_____	_____
_____	_____	_____

Factors of Production

DIRECTIONS: List each factor of production in the box where you think it BEST FITS.

Resources (natural and man-made):	Labor:	Capital:

Which category do you think will cost you the most money? Why?

How could you go about getting what you need to open your business?

What else do you think is needed to make a business succeed?

Why do you think many businesses fail in the first few years?

A Leap of Faith

Springboard:
>   Students should read and complete the "GIANTS in Their Fields" handout.
>   *(Answers may vary, but all are successful entrepreneurs - introduce term.)*

Objective: The student will be able to explain how entrepreneurs succeed.

Materials:	GIANTS in Their Fields (Springboard handout) The Next Best Thing (handout) Checking out the Competition (multiple 1/2 page handouts – see Procedures) art supplies and butcher (or other large) paper
Terms to know:	**entrepreneur** - person who opens and runs a business **advertise** - make goods and services known **competition** - similar businesses vying for consumers

Procedure:

- During discussion of Springboard, explain that *successful entrepreneurs usually offer good quality products or services that people need or want, then advertise to make their business known, and provide good service*. Go on to explain that *in this lesson the student(s) will continue to examine the business sector.* (**NOTE:** You may need to either allot additional days for this project or reduce the requirements to fit one class.)

- Distribute "The Next Best Thing" and art supplies and review the directions. The student(s) should answer the questions and complete the poster as instructed in Steps 1-3 (leaving Step 4 blank) individually, in pairs, or groups.

- Have them display their work and distribute "Checking out the Competition." The student(s) should complete one survey **FOR EACH** project. **Individual projects** can be evaluated by the teacher or parent and family members.

- Collect and give the feedback to each student or group to complete Step 4 of the project handout.

- Lead a discussion including the following questions:
  - ? What do you think would be good about being an entrepreneur? *(Answers may vary: being your own boss, possibly getting rich, getting to be creative, getting famous, etc.)*
  - ? What might be bad about being an entrepreneur? *(Answers will vary: losing your money and time if your business doesn't succeed, etc.)*
  - ? What do you think determines if an entrepreneur succeeds or fails? *(Answers will vary; success depends on how good an idea is, if people need it or want to buy it, if it is advertised well, etc.)*
  - ? Entrepreneurship is sometimes called the fourth factor of production. Do you think entrepreneurs are a necessary part of the business sector? *(Answers may vary but should be explained.)*
  - ? What advice would you offer someone wanting to be an entrepreneur? *(Answers may vary: work hard; be persistent; etc.)*

GIANTS in Their Fields

"I had to pick myself up and get on with it, do it all over again, only even better this time."
Sam Walton, founder of Walmart

"The important thing is not being afraid to take a chance. Remember the greatest failure is to not try. Once you find something you love to do, be the best at doing it."
Debbie Fields, founder of Mrs. Field's Cookies

"Our success has really been based on partnerships from the very beginning."
Bill Gates, founder of Microsoft

"When you reach an obstacle, turn it into an opportunity… You can overcome and be a winner, or you can allow it to overcome you and be a loser. Refuse to throw in the towel."
Mary Kay Ash, founder of Mary Kay Cosmetics

What are some things these people all have in common?

What words would you use to describe these people?

Do you think they are successful? Why or why not?

The Next Be$t Thing!

Congratulations! You are in a contest to find the next great entrepreneur. Answer the questions and follow the directions to develop, advertise, and present your product.

Step One: Develop Your Product
1. What is/are your idea(s) for a new good or service?

2. How would this fill a need?

3. Who would buy it?

4. Who would be your competition?

5. How much will you charge for this good or service?

Step Two: What Are the Risks?
1. What will you need to open your business?

2. Where will you get the money and everything else you need?

3. What will happen if your product doesn't sell?

Step Three: Present Your Product
Create a poster that introduces your product and will get customers to buy it. Your poster should include:
·   packaging - draw a picture of the product
·   catchy and clever slogan
·   a logo or trademark people will remember
·   ad that will draw attention to your product

Step Four: Evaluate Your Work
What do you think you did very well?

What could you have improved on?

Do you think your business would succeed or fail? Why?

CHECKING OUT THE COMPETITION

Product evaluation for: _____

Circle your choice for each question

There is a need for this product.	Agree	Not sure	Disagree
The price of this product is good.	Agree	Not sure	Disagree
The packaging is attractive.	Agree	Not sure	Disagree
The slogan is catchy.	Agree	Not sure	Disagree
The logo / trademark will make me remember this product.	Agree	Not sure	Disagree
The ad makes me want the product.	Agree	Not sure	Disagree
I would DEFINITELY buy this!	Agree	Not sure	Disagree

COMMENTS:

CHECKING OUT THE COMPETITION

Product evaluation for: _____

Circle your choice for each question

There is a need for this product.	Agree	Not sure	Disagree
The price of this product is good.	Agree	Not sure	Disagree
The packaging is attractive.	Agree	Not sure	Disagree
The slogan is catchy.	Agree	Not sure	Disagree
The logo / trademark will make me remember this product.	Agree	Not sure	Disagree
The ad makes me want the product.	Agree	Not sure	Disagree
I would DEFINITELY buy this!	Agree	Not sure	Disagree

COMMENTS:

Getting What You Want

Springboard:

Students should read the "Striking a Deal" skit in pairs and answer the questions.

Objective: The student will be able to explain how supply and demand works between consumers and sellers.

Materials:

Striking a Deal (Springboard handout)
Goods Cards (card cut-outs)
Task Cards (1/3-page card cut-outs per group)
Ye Ole Trade Simulation (handout or transparency)
So What Does it All Mean? (handout)

Terms to know:

barter - dealing back and forth to come to an agreement
supply - amount of a good or service that can be bought
demand - level of need or want for a good or service

Procedure:

· During discussion of the Springboard, explain that _the two students making offers back and forth to work out their trade is a process called "barter." Both students were looking out for themselves, trying to get what THEY wanted_. Go on to explain that _in this lesson the student(s) will learn more about barter_.

· **NOTE:** This activity is a simulation best done in groups. Have students work in sixes, assigning each a role: farmer, candle maker, blacksmith, butcher, trapper, or doctor. Give each student the Goods and Task cards that go with his/her role. **For individualized instruction** the simulation should be done when a group opportunity arises, if not 6 then as many as possible. (If fewer, leave out one or more parts as needed.)

· Review the directions for "Ye Ole Trade Simulation" and have the students work for 10-15 minutes to complete their tasks.

· Then distribute "So What Does it All Mean?" and have them respond to the reflection questions.

· Have the student(s) share and compare their answers and discuss. (**NOTE:** The teacher answer page provides a guide for discussion and introduction of lesson terms.)

Student 1: I just got some new superhero trading cards. I'll trade you my Captain Amazing for your Princess of Power.

Student 2: Why would I want a Captain Amazing card? I already have three of those. Everyone has those anyway. I'll trade you my Princess of Power for your Superboy card.

Student 1: No way! I only have one of those and they're REALLY hard to get. What about an Amazing Man? You don't have any of those.

Student 2: Hmmm. That's true. I really want a Superboy, but I guess the Amazing Man would be good, too. But those aren't nearly as hard to get as the Superboy cards. You'll have to throw in something else.

Student 1: O.K. What about a Greta the Great? I have two of those, but they're cool.

Student 2: Alright, you've got a deal.

What did each student bring to trade in this skit? _____

_____

Who had the most valuable item(s)? How do you know? _____

_____

_____

Why didn't Student 2 want to trade at first? What did you think of that reason? ____

_____

_____

What made some cards more valuable than others? _____

_____

_____

How might this deal have been different if both students had several of each kind of card? _____

_____

_____

Student 1: I just got some new superhero trading cards. I'll trade you my Captain Amazing for your Princess of Power.

Student 2: Why would I want a Captain Amazing card? I already have three of those. Everyone has those anyway. I'll trade you my Princess of Power for your Superboy card.

Student 1: No way! I only have one of those and they're REALLY hard to get. What about an Amazing Man? You don't have any of those.

Student 2: Hmmm. That's true. I really want a Superboy, but I guess the Amazing Man would be good, too. But those aren't nearly as hard to get as the Superboy cards. You'll have to throw in something else.

Student 1: O.K. What about a Greta the Great? I have two of those, but they're cool.

Student 2: Alright, you've got a deal.

What did each student bring to trade in this situation? *Student 1 brought Captain Amazing, Superboy, Amazing Man, and Greta the Great cards to the trade. Student 2 brought a Princess of Power card.*

Who had the most valuable item(s)? How do you know? *Answers may vary but should be explained. It could be argued that either the Princess Power or Superboy cards were the most valuable because both students wanted them and neither student wanted to give them up.*

Why did Student 2 not want to trade at first? Do you think that was a good reason? *Student 2 didn't want to trade because what was offered was not valuable to him/her. S(he) argued that the card in question (Captain Amazing) was easy to get. It is often true that products that are scarce become more valuable, a concept addressed further in this lesson and the next.*

Why were some of these cards more valuable than others? *The value of the various cards seemed to depend on how many there were available. If they were easy to get, it was likely the student had more than one of them, so they were less valued. If cards were rare, the students didn't want to give them up.*

How might this deal have been different if both students had several of each kind of card? *Answers may vary but trades wouldn't have been necessary if each student had plenty of each card. The purpose of the trades is to get what you don't have while giving up as little as possible.*

Goods Ω Cards

Farmer **EGGS**	Farmer **EGGS**	Farmer **EGGS**
Farmer **EGGS**	Farmer **EGGS**	Farmer **CORN**
Farmer **CORN**	Farmer **CORN**	Farmer **CORN**
Farmer **CORN**	Farmer **CORN**	Farmer **EGGS**
Blacksmith **HORSESHOES**	Blacksmith **HORSESHOES**	Blacksmith **HORSESHOES**
Candle Maker **CANDLES**	Candle Maker **CANDLES**	Candle Maker **CANDLES**
Candle Maker **CANDLES**	Trapper **FURS**	Trapper **FURS**
Doctor **MEDICINE**	Butcher **MEAT**	Butcher **MEAT**

Task ∩ Cards

Farmer You need candles, medicine, and horseshoes.	**Candle Maker** You need eggs, medicine, and meat.	**Butcher** You need grain, medicine, and candles.
Blacksmith You need candles, medicine, and fur.	**Doctor** You need candles, fur, and eggs.	**Trapper** You need medicine, eggs, corn, and horseshoes.

Farmer You need candles, medicine, and horseshoes.	**Candle Maker** You need eggs, medicine, and meat.	**Butcher** You need grain, medicine, and candles.
Blacksmith You need candles, medicine, and fur.	**Doctor** You need candles, fur, and eggs.	**Trapper** You need medicine, eggs, corn, and horseshoes.

Farmer You need candles, medicine, and horseshoes.	**Candle Maker** You need eggs, medicine, and meat.	**Butcher** You need grain, medicine, and candles.
Blacksmith You need candles, medicine, and fur.	**Doctor** You need candles, fur, and eggs.	**Trapper** You need medicine, eggs, corn, and horseshoes.

Ye Ole Trade Simulation

DIRECTIONS:

Each person in your group has a role: farmer, candle maker, blacksmith, trapper, doctor or butcher. You will get cards that tell you what you have to trade. You will also be given a card that says what you need from the others.

RULES

1. Everyone must show good manners in the marketplace. No running or shouting.

2. You can only trade with one other person at a time. You should not try to deal with someone who is already talking to another person.

3. You can continue to barter as long as the market is open. You can make as many trades as you wish.

4. Be aware that everyone has different items to sell and different things they need.

5. You can only trade items that you have on your cards.

6. You can make several trades with the same person.

7. Any problems must be settled by the teacher. The teacher's word is final.

8. When the market closes, you must stop trading right away. Take your cards back to your seat and wait to be told what to do next.

So What Does it All Mean?

1. Were you able to trade for everything you wanted? Why or why not?

   _____

   _____

   _____

2. Were there items that **NO ONE** wanted? Why do you think this was the
   case?_____

   _____

   _____

3. Were there any items that **EVERYONE** wanted? Were you able to
   barter for these items? Explain._____

   _____

   _____

   _____

4. Which "person" do you think did **BEST** in the simulation? Why?_____

   _____

   _____

   _____

5. Who do you think made out the **WORST** in the simulation? Why?_____

   _____

   _____

   _____

6. How do you think this simulation might have been different if everyone
   used money to buy things?_____

   _____

   _____

   _____

7. Based on the simulation, explain what you think this statement means:
   "When something is in short supply, it will be more in demand." _____

   _____

   _____

   _____

   _____

So What Does it All Mean?
Suggestions for Answers and Explanations

1. Were you able to trade for everything you wanted? Why or why not? *Answers will vary depending on the role of the student. It is likely that most were not able to get everything they needed, either because there wasn't enough for everybody (as was the case with medicine) or no one had it at all (such as grain).*

2. Were there items that **NO ONE** wanted? Why do you think this was the case? *The farmer would have had the hardest time getting rid of all his/her corn and eggs. Only a few others wanted these items and (s)he had a lot of both of these goods. At this point introduce the term "supply" and ask student(s) to explain how much supply of these items the farmer had. Have them explain whether the supply for these items was high or low. (high)*

3. Were there any items that **EVERYONE** wanted? Were you able to barter for these items? Explain. *The doctor had medicine that EVERYONE wanted. The candle maker also had candles that several others wanted. It was very difficult to get these items because there was only one person who had them, there were few of them, and everyone wanted them. Introduce the term "demand" and have the student(s) explain whether these items were in high or low demand (high) and if the supply was high or low. (low)*

4. Which "person" do you think did **BEST** in the simulation? Why? *Answers will vary, but it is likely that the doctor and candle maker both made out well because they had the items in high demand and could probably "get" more in trade for them.*

5. Who do you think made out the **WORST** in the simulation? Why? *Answers will vary but anyone who didn't get what they wanted did not do well.*

6. How do you think this simulation might have been different if everyone used money to buy things? *Money would have made the simulation easier. Assuming that everyone started with the same amount of money, everyone would have started on equal footing, as opposed to some people having almost useless goods (such as the farmer) trying to trade with someone who had something very valuable (as the doctor).*

7. Based on the simulation, explain what you think this statement means: "When something is in short supply, it will be more in demand." *Answers will vary somewhat, but should be logical based on the simulation. (More on this concept in the next lesson.)*

Objective: The student will be able to explain how price affects supply and demand of goods and services.

Materials: Money, Money, Money (Springboard handout)
                    Figure It Out (handout)
                    It's the Laws (handout)

Terms to know: **currency** - anything used to pay for goods and services
                    money - most-used form of currency; bills and coins

Procedure:

· While reviewing the Springboard, point out that *after money was invented and came into common use, buying and selling goods and services became MUCH easier*. Go on to explain that *in this lesson, the student(s) will examine the pricing of goods and services*.

· Distribute "Figure It Out," review the directions, and have the student(s) complete the handout individually, in pairs, or small groups.

· Have them share their ideas. *(Answers may vary but in general, highly valued or rare items cost more than those that are more common or easy to get.)*

· Then distribute "It's the Laws." Explain that *price and the supply and demand for goods and services are closely related*. Have the student(s) read the information and then make predictions based on the laws of supply and demand. *(Answers may vary if well-reasoned, but possibilities include:*

1. *The price will be cut since the demand fell after the holiday.*
2. *The prices will likely be reduced since there is so much supply.*
3. *The nail salon could charge more since the supply is so low, unless demand is also low. On the other hand higher prices could make women forego the "luxury" of having their nails done at all.*
4. *Any stores that DO have the toy can increase the price, since demand is so high and supply is so low.*
5. *Again, any gas stations in the area that DO have gas could raise the price since demand is high and supplies are low. (However many places have laws against "price gouging," taking advantage of people in emergencies.)*
6. *This one is a bit tougher. It is possible that if many people want the dog, the price of Labs will go up. On the other hand, it may be that so many people have the dog BECAUSE they cost less than most rare breeds.*
7. *This could also be viewed in different ways. According to the law of supply, it would be expected that the boys would each have to charge less since several offer the service. But it's more likely that they all charge about the same and people are willing to pay a fair price for kids performing the service.)*

$$$ Money, Money, Money $$$

   Throughout history, people have bartered and made other deals to get what they needed. Farmers would take the food they grew to the village blacksmith for a pair of horseshoes. But trading one good for another can cause problems. For example if the farmer went to the blacksmith, who already had enough eggs, the trade would not work out. The farmer could not get what he needs, because he didn't have what the blacksmith wants. Also, carrying around eggs and other goods while shopping can be a tricky! And think about trade with other towns!

   In some communities, **currency** came into use to solve these problems. Coins or other small items of value were so much simpler to carry! Currency is anything with value used to buy goods and services. In olden times, people used shells or beads. Coins were in use as early as 700 B.C. Later the ancient Greeks and Romans also used coins. It took a long time, though, for coins to make their way around the world. Even in colonial America people bartered for what they needed and wanted.

   After America won its freedom, Congress passed the Mint Act in 1792. This law made the dollar the currency of the United States. The first coins were made in Philadelphia a year later. Paper money, though, was not used in the U.S. until the 1800's. It came into use because the government needed to quickly print money to pay for the Civil War. "Greenbacks" were first printed in 1861 and are still used today.

Which sentence is **MOST LIKELY** about barter?
   A. Max gave Eli three cookies in his lunch for a candy bar.
   B. Abby gave her sister her sweat shirt when she grew out of it.
   C. Sam and Marty split a sandwich at Big John's up the block.
   D. Erica took her book bag to school but came home without it.

Which word means **MOST NEARLY** the same thing as "currency"?
   A. goods   B. money   C. shells   D. dollar

Which statement shows how currency solved problems?
   A. "I have a cow and horse from this town to take to the next."
   B. "These two bags of wheat should be enough to get shoes!"
   C. "I can carry all I need to buy goods in my pockets."
   D. "What am I going to do with five wooden barrels?"

Based on the reading, it can be said that coins were first used in
   A. ancient times.   B. Greece.   C. Rome.   D. America.

Fill in the blanks so this sentence makes sense.

Barter is _____, while currency is _____.

Throughout history, people have bartered and made other deals to get what they needed. Farmers would take the food they grew to the village blacksmith for a pair of horseshoes. But trading one good for another can cause problems. For example if the farmer went to the blacksmith, who already had enough eggs, the trade would not work out. The farmer could not get what he needs, because he didn't have what the blacksmith wants. Also, carrying around eggs and other goods while shopping can be a tricky! And think about trade with other towns!

In some communities, **currency** came into use to solve these problems. Coins or other small items of value were so much simpler to carry! Currency is anything with value used to buy goods and services. In olden times, people used shells or beads. Coins were in use as early as 700 B.C. Later the ancient Greeks and Romans also used coins. It took a long time, though, for coins to make their way around the world. Even in colonial America people bartered for what they needed and wanted.

After America won its freedom, Congress passed the Mint Act in 1792. This law made the dollar the currency of the United States. The first coins were made in Philadelphia a year later. Paper money, though, was not used in the U.S. until the 1800's. It came into use because the government needed to quickly print money to pay for the Civil War. "Greenbacks" were first printed in 1861 and are still used today.

Which sentence is **MOST LIKELY** about barter?
    A. Max gave Eli three cookies in his lunch for a candy bar. *
    B. Abby gave her sister her sweat shirt when she grew out of it.
    C. Sam and Marty split a sandwich at Big John's up the block.
    D. Erica took her book bag to school but came home without it.
    (Choices B and C illustrate sharing and D loss or forgetfulness. A involved a trade of one thing for another.)

Which word means **MOST NEARLY** the same thing as "currency"?
    A. goods   B. money *   C. shells   D. dollar
    (Choice A is bought with currency. Though other things besides money can be currency, C and D are examples of items used as money.)

Which statement shows how currency solved problems?
    A. "I have a cow and horse from this town to take to the next."
    B. "These two bags of wheat should be enough to get shoes!"
    C. "I can carry all I need to buy goods in my pockets." *
    D. "What am I going to do with five wooden barrels?"
    (Convenience and portability are two ways currency improved trade.)

Based on the reading, it can be said that coins were first used in
    A. ancient times.*   B. Greece.   C. Rome.   D. America.
    (Though Choice A is not stated, B, C, and D are false based on the reading.)

Fill in the blanks so this sentence makes sense.
Barter is _____, while currency is _____.
(Answers may vary but should make sense based on the reading.)

FIGURE IT OUT

Which Costs More? And Why?

DIRECTIONS: For each pair of items, tell which would cost more and explain why. Then make up two pairs of items of your own. Explain which in each pair would cost more and why.

A diamond? or a piece of gravel?

The Superbowl M.V.P.? or the third string quarterback?

A 1969 Classic Corvette?   or a 2000 Ford Focus?

Tickets to a sold out concert? or tickets to the local theater?

Your example:

Your example:

IT'S THE LAWS

The Law of Supply:	The Law of Demand:
• When the supply goes down, the price goes up. • When supply goes up, the price goes down.	• If the demand goes up, the price goes up. • If the demand goes down, the price goes down.

DIRECTIONS: Based on the laws of supply and demand, tell what you think will happen to the prices of the **goods** or **services** in each case. Explain your ideas.

1. After Mother's Day, a local florist has several dozen **roses** left that she didn't sell.

2. During back to school time, every store in the city has **backpacks** for sale.

3. The local mall has only one **nail salon**. The next closest one is over 20 miles away.

4. The hottest toy this Christmas is **a new video game**. All stores in town are sold out.

5. A hurricane has damaged hundreds of oil rigs in the Gulf of Mexico. It will be weeks before **gasoline** trucks will be able to supply gas stations.

6. The most popular dog in America for five years in a row has been the **Labrador Retriever**. Three times as many families own this breed than others.

7. There are several twelve year old boys living in the Brookdale subdivision who **mow lawns** for extra money.

Who You Gonna Call?

Springboard:
   Students should study the "Yellow Pages" handout
   and answer the questions.

Objective: The student will be able to explain how competition affects the business sector.

Materials: Yellow Pages (Springboard handout)
                             Standing Out (2-page handout)
                             Yellow Pages, Yellow Book, or other business directories (optional)

Terms to know: **industry** - the whole of all businesses offering the same product or service (ex. the hotel industry)
                             monopoly - when only one business offers a good or service with NO competition

Procedure:

· After reviewing the Springboard, explain that _in decks and patios as in other industries, there is usually competition -- other businesses that offer the same goods or services. Some industries have HEAVY competition, others have a little, and a few called monopolies have none._ (introduce term) _Depending upon the level of competition, businesses have to make themselves stand out in the crowd._ Have the student(s) suggest ways businesses can stand out. _(Advertise, offer specials, give great service, etc.)_ Go on to explain that _this lesson looks at competition and how the business sector handles it._

· Distribute "Standing Out" and review the directions. Have the student(s) work individually, in pairs, or groups to consider each industry and decide the level of competition involved in it. If available, the student(s) could use a local business directory or a local Internet directory to look up each topic to see how many listings are shown. They could also simply use their own knowledge of their location.

· Have the students or groups share their ideas and discuss. _(Answers may vary widely with location. Small towns may have only one large department store, while big cities may have several. Overall, though, gas stations and restaurants will likely have the most competition. Cable and electric companies are near-monopolies, and others fall in between. Student suggestions for standing out in each industry will vary but should make sense and reflect an understanding of the need for businesses to promote themselves, particularly if their industry has a high level of competition.)_

YELLOW PAGES

 PATIOS AND DECKS BLDRS

Acme Builders 21884 Park St...554-8220
Al's Patios   1602 E. Main St....555-0301
Garden Deck and Patio
          611 Simpson St..........525-8855

M **Metro Patios**
Be the envy of your neighbors!
Call the **BIG M** today!
Mention this ad for 10% off
3898 Stillwell Rd.
552-2222

Mack's Decks 16 Elm Ave....551-1785
Nat 'n Sam Builders

PRESTIGE
DECK & PATIO
Let our 18 years of experience
change your home! We do it all!
Stone, wood, brick …
you name it, we'll do it!

Call 551-1000
for a free quote!

Royalty Custom Patios
THE KING OF CONCRETE!
          4462 8th St. Hpvl......612-7334

The company called _____ most likely receives the most calls because _____.
    A. Acme builders … its first on the list
    B. Metro Patios … it offers people 10% off
    C. Prestige Deck & Patio … has a big, bold ad
    D. Royalty Custom Patios … of its clever slogan

"BLDRS" on the top line **MOST LIKELY**
    A. means "big leading deck repair services."
    B. is an abbreviation for the word "builders."
    C. was added to "patios and decks" to fill space.
    D. tells this page has more listings from the last.

Based on this "Yellow Page," it can be said that
    A. it is part of a book of business listings.
    B. "Yellow Pages" only list deck companies.
    C. deck companies made a flyer together.
    D. everyone wants a new deck or patio built.

Based on this page, what kinds of things can companies do to make their business stand out? _____

_____

_____

What efforts do you think work **BEST**, and why? _____

_____

_____

 PATIOS AND DECKS BLDRS

Acme Builders 21884 Park St...554-8220
Al's Patios 1602 E. Main St....555-0301
Garden Deck and Patio
        611 Simpson St...........525-8855

M **Metro Patios**
Be the envy of your neighbors!
Call the **BIG M** today!
Mention this ad for 10% off
3898 Stillwell Rd.
552-2222

Mack's Decks 16 Elm Ave......551-1785
Nat 'n Sam Builders

PRESTIGE
DECK & PATIO
Let our 18 years of experience
change your home! We do it all!
Stone, wood, brick …
you name it, we'll do it!

Call 551-1000
for a free quote!

Royalty Custom Patios
THE KING OF CONCRETE!
        4462 8th St. Hpvl......612-7334

The company called ____ most likely receives the most calls because ____.
    A. Acme builders … its first on the list
    B. Metro Patios … it offers people 10% off
    C. Prestige Deck & Patio … has a big, bold ad *
    D. Royalty Custom Patios … of its clever slogan

(B is arguably also a good choice, but MOST LIKELY the big ad attracts people. Prestige also has 18 years experience, which has appeal.)

"BLDRS" on the top line **MOST LIKELY**
    A. means "big leading deck repair services."
    B. is an abbreviation for the word "builders." *
    C. was added to "patios and decks" to fill space.
    D. tells this page has more listings from the last.

(Choice C is clearly wrong, and D is false since it's the heading of a new category. B is the most logical option.)

Based on this "Yellow Page," it can be said that
    A. it is part of a book of business listings. *
    B. "Yellow Pages" only list deck companies.
    C. deck companies made a flyer together.
    D. everyone wants a new deck or patio built.

(Many students will likely have seen Yellow Pages or advertisements for them. If so, Choice A is really the only good one.)

Based on this page, what kinds of things can companies do to make their business stand out? *Answers may vary somewhat and include: list in business directories, advertise, offer discounts, make up memorable slogans, try to give customers confidence in the company's experience, etc.*

What efforts do you think work **BEST**, and why? *Answers may of course vary, but should be explained and make sense.*

STANDING OUT

DIRECTIONS: For each industry, mark an <u>X</u> on the line to show how much competition there is in it. Then below each, think of at least one thing YOU could do if you owned a business in that industry to REALLY make it stand out.

Gas station:

Monopoly ————————————————————————→ Heavy
Competition

Toy store:

Monopoly ————————————————————————→ Heavy
Competition

Cable Company:

Monopoly ————————————————————————→ Heavy
Competition

Restaurant:

Monopoly ————————————————————————→ Heavy
Competition

Discount Store:

Monopoly ————————————————————————→ Heavy
Competition

Gymnastics Studio:

Monopoly ●————————————————————→ Heavy Competition

Electric Company:

Monopoly ●————————————————————→ Heavy Competition

Vet:

Monopoly ●————————————————————→ Heavy Competition

Book Store:

Monopoly ●————————————————————→ Heavy Competition

Car Dealer:

Monopoly ●————————————————————→ Heavy Competition

Movie Theater:

Monopoly ●————————————————————→ Heavy Competition

Break it Down!

> **Springboard:**
> Students should read "_____" and answer the questions.

Objective: The student will be able to explain how specialization has influenced production.

Materials:	"_____ " (Springboard handout)
	"Booking" It (2 page handout)
	scrap paper (a pile per group)
	yarn (or string) and rulers
	scissors (one set per group)
	rubber bands (several per group)
	"Assembling" Results (handout)

Terms to know:	**production** - making goods
	assembly line - a system of production where workers complete just one part of assembly
	specialization - doing one task well
	technology - ways to make work easier and faster

Procedure:

- During discussion of the Springboard, have the student(s) predict some of the advantages and disadvantages of mass production. *(Advantages include: faster, cheaper goods consumers can buy for less. Disadvantages may include: worker boredom, need for close inspections, etc.)* Go on to explain that <u>in this lesson the student(s) will learn more about mass production.</u>

- **NOTE:** Once again this activity is a simulation which lends itself to group work. Have students work in threes or **for individualized instruction,** either do the activity when a group opportunity arises or time the student making the books alone and with you; then he/she can make inferences about production rates with more workers.

- Distribute the book-making supplies (not the rubber band) and the "'Booking' It" handout. Review the directions and have the student(s) complete each round, timing them so each is exactly the same length (about 5-7 minutes should be enough). Allow time after each round for them to count their books, record their information, and calculate their profits. For Round 3 distribute rubber bands and proceed as with the other two.

- Then distribute ""Assembling' Results." Review the last two terms and have the student(s) complete the analysis based on their simulation experience.

- Have them share their results and analyses and discuss. *(Answers may vary, but the following points should be noted:*
  - *Assembly lines and specialization makes production faster and cheaper*
  - *Businesses are always looking for new technologies to improve production and profits.*
  - *Specialization can make work faster, but if jobs disappear due to new technology or other reasons, workers must learn new skills to find jobs.*

For the business sector to make money, goods or services must be offered. Companies that make goods want to make as many as fast as they can. They also want to produce goods at the lowest cost. **Mass** production, or making large amounts of product quickly, is the answer.

The first businesses to use mass production were mines in the Middle Ages (500-1500 AD). Workers would pass pots of rocks down long lines to remove it quickly. Later, business owners used assembly lines. Products were built in pieces with each worker doing just one task.

Meat-packing companies were the first to use assembly lines. Workers would each cut off one piece of an animal as it passed by them. Then in 1913, Henry Ford had the idea to use the assembly line to make Model T cars. Ford said the meat-packing lines gave him the idea.

Each person on an assembly line is responsible for adding one part to the car or other product. Since they only had one job, they were very good at that task. The system proved to be a great success! In the case of the Model T, the time to build the car fell from over 12 hours to just an hour-and-a-half! Because the car was made faster and less costly to build, Ford could charge less for his Model T's!

Which would be the **BEST** title for the reading?
    A. "Making More Money in Business"
    B. "The History of Mass Production"
    C. "Henry Ford and the Car Business"
    D. "Miners and Meat Packers."

The word "mass" as it is used in the reading **MOST NEARLY** means a
    A. Catholic church service.   C. huge number.
    B. large lump or tumor.   D. large crowd.

Which picture **BEST** shows how an assembly line works?

A.    C.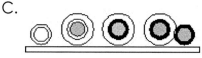

B. 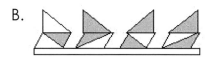   D.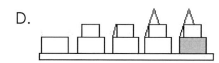

Which of these statements is **MOST LIKELY** true based on the reading?
    A. Europe was ahead of America in mass production.
    B. Henry Ford was the first to make use of assembly lines.
    C. Mass production allows goods to be sold at lower prices.
    D. Assembly lines made Model T's faster, but quality was poor.

For the business sector to make money, goods or services must be offered. Companies that make goods want to make as many as fast as they can. They also want to produce goods at the lowest cost. **Mass** production, or making large amounts of product quickly, is the answer.

The first businesses to use mass production were mines in the Middle Ages (500-1500 AD). Workers would pass pots of rocks down long lines to remove it quickly. Later, business owners used assembly lines. Products were built in pieces with each worker doing just one task.

Meat-packing companies were the first to use assembly lines. Workers would each cut off one piece of an animal as it passed by them. Then in 1913, Henry Ford had the idea to use the assembly line to make Model T cars. Ford said the meat-packing lines gave him the idea.

Each person on an assembly line is responsible for adding one part to the car or other product. Since they only had one job, they were very good at that task. The system proved to be a great success! In the case of the Model T, the time to build the car fell from over 12 hours to just an hour-and-a-half! Because the car was made faster and less costly to build, Ford could charge less for his Model T's!

Which would be the **BEST** title for the reading?
    A. "Making More Money in Business"
    B. "The History of Mass Production" *
    C. "Henry Ford and the Car Business"
    D. "Miners and Meat Packers."

(Choices C and D are details about the history, and though mass production was begun as ONE MEANS of making more money, Choice B is the best.)

The word "mass" as it is used in the reading **MOST NEARLY** means a
    A. Catholic church service.   C. large number. *
    B. large lump or tumor.   D. huge crowd.
    (The sentence says mass production allowed for "large amounts of product" to be made quickly.)

Which picture **BEST** shows how an assembly line works?
A.    C.

B.    D. *

(Choice D is the only one that shows one change from each station to the next.)

Which of these statements is **TRUE** based on the reading?
    A. Europe was ahead of America in mass production.
    B. Henry Ford was the first to make use of assembly lines.
    C. Mass production allows goods to be sold at lower prices. *
    D. Assembly lines made Model T's faster, but quality was poor.
    (The Middle Ages information is not sufficient to choose A, and B and D are false. The Model T was a HUGE success! C is true, which is why it is still used.)

"BOOKING" It!

DIRECTIONS: You are a worker in a book factory. Your boss is working on ways to make more books, cheaper and faster. You and your team are helping with an experiment.

Complete each round below and follow the directions given for it. Work fast but keep up a steady pace in all rounds. Your work speed should not make the difference from round to round. After time is called for each round, fill in the Production Log on the next page.

You will also need to figure the profit in each round. The point of the experiment is to make books faster and <u>CHEAPER</u>, so cost is important! The costs of "parts" and tools for making the books are:

> Piece of paper - $1
> Scissors - $1
> Ruler - $1
> 12 inches of string - $1
> Rubber band - $1

* Each book sells for $7.00. Use this number to figure out your profit.

ROUND 1 - Everyone on your team should make the books. All should follow steps 1-5. Use the drawings below to help.
1. Fold three pieces of paper in half. (A)
2. Place the papers inside each other. (B)
3. Cut a small notch at either end of the fold to make two holes. (C)
4. Measure a 12 inch piece of string and cut it. (D)
5. Thread the string through the holes. (E)
6. Tie a bow to hold the pages together and trim any extra string. (F)

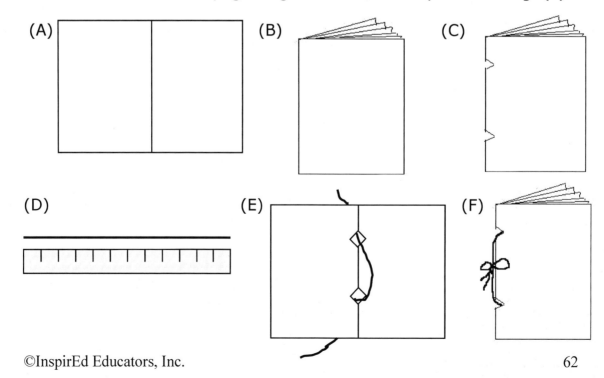

ROUND 2 – The books will be made in the same way. But team members should split up the tasks as follows:

Team member #1 - Fold three pieces of paper and place them inside each other. (A & B)

Team member #2 - Cut the notches and 7 inch piece of string. (C & D)

Team member #3 – Thread and tie the string. (E & F)

* Each member should do only his/her "job" nonstop the whole time. After the first book, all should do their jobs until told to stop.

ROUND 3 - Again, team members will split up the tasks, this time as follows:

Team member #1 - Fold three pieces of paper. (A)

Team member #2 - Place the papers inside each other. (B)

NOTE: DO NOT DO STEPS 3-6 AS BEFORE!

Team member #3 – Instead stretch a rubber band around the pages at the fold to bind the book pages together as shown.

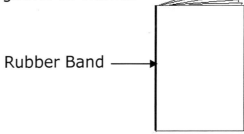

Rubber Band ⟶

* As in Round 2, all should do ONLY their own jobs nonstop.

PRODUCTION LOG

	ROUND 1	ROUND 2	ROUND 3
Number of books made			
Books made per worker			
Earnings (total books times $7)			
Total Costs (add up costs per book and multiply by number of books made)			
Total Profit (earnings minus total costs)			

"ASSEMBLING" RESULTS

1. Which round produced the fewest books? Why? _____
   _____
   _____

2. Which round produced the most books? Why? _____
   _____
   _____

3. Which round do you think made the best use of labor? Explain. _____
   _____
   _____
   _____

4. How did new technology (the rubber band) change the production?
   Explain. _____
   _____
   _____

5. How did specialization affect production? Explain. _____
   _____
   _____

6. In what ways do you think "specializing" in one job would be good for
   industry and workers? In what ways might it hurt? _____
   _____
   _____
   _____

7. Give an example of how the production of something today shows an
   idea from the lesson. _____
   _____
   _____

For the People

Springboard:
Students should complete the
"Community Care' brainstorming form.
(Answers may vary: police, firemen, air traffic controllers, doctors, teachers, etc.)

Objective: The student will be able to describe the role of the government sector in an economy.

Materials: Community Care (Springboard handout)
                          What CAN Your Government Do for You? (handout)

Terms to know: **taxes** - money paid to the government to pay for government services and other costs

Procedure:

·   During discussion of the Springboard, explain that *many of the people who help in a community work for the government.* Review the student(s)' lists with them, having them highlight or circle any community helpers that ARE government workers. Then go on to explain that *the government is one of the four sectors of our economy. This lesson examines ways the government is involved in the economy, not only in the local community but at the state and national levels as well.*

·   Distribute the "What CAN Your Government Do for You?" survey. Explain that this list includes some of the services the government provides. Have the student(s) fill in the chart individually or with a partner. (**NOTE:** It may be necessary to generally explain what some items on the list mean.)

·   Have them share their answers *(Suggestions below, but may vary)*, rankings, and reasoning. Include the following questions in the follow-up discussion:

    ? Who should pay for these services? *(Answers may vary; the students will likely say the government should pay though.)*

    ? Where does the government get the money to pay for these services? *(If not mentioned, explain that tax dollars fund the government.)*

    ? In what other way(s) does the government affect our economy? *(It helps other sectors of the economy, protects consumers, guards people's safety, etc. Also, by using so many goods, the government is an important consumer, as well as providing MANY jobs; etc.)*

Police	L, S	Post Office	L, N	Jails, Prisons	L, S, N
Fire Dept.	L	Museums	L, S, N	Foreign Affairs	N
Schools	L, S, N	Parks	L, S, N	Trade	L, S, N
Buses, Rails	L, N	Environment	L, S, N	Aged	L, S, N
Child Protect.	L, S, N	Consumers	L, S, N	Trash	L
Libraries	L, N	Med. Research	L, S, N	Fair Treatment	L, S, N
Roads	L, S, N	Poor	L, S, N	Patents	N
911	L	Air Traffic	N	Help World	N
Motor Veh.	L, S	Currency	N	Borders	N
Courts	L, S, N	Rec. Activities	L, S, N	Weather Svc.	L, S, N
Army, etc.	S, N	Emergency Aid	L, S, N	Dams, Bridges	L, S, N

COMMUNITY CARE

DIRECTIONS: Brainstorm a list of EVERYONE you can think of who HELPS in your community in some way.

_____   _____

_____   _____

_____   _____

_____   _____

_____   _____

_____   _____

_____   _____

_____   _____

_____   _____

_____   _____

_____   _____

_____   _____

_____   _____

_____   _____

_____   _____

WHAT CAN YOUR GOVERNMENT DO FOR YOU?

DIRECTIONS: Below is a list of services that government provides. For each, tell whether it affects: the <u>local</u> community, town, or city; <u>state</u>; or <u>nation</u> (or more than one?). Then <u>RATE</u> its importance from 1 (NOT important) to 10 (VERY important). Be ready to explain your ideas. List any other government services you think of at the end.

SERVICE	Local, State, or Nation	RATING	SERVICE	Local, State, or Nation	RATING
Police Department			Air Traffic Control		
Fire Department			Currency		
Public Schools			Recreation Activities		
Buses and Rails			Help in Emergencies		
Protect Children			Jails and Prisons		
Libraries			Foreign Affairs		
Roads and Highways			Control of Trade		
911 Service			Care for the Aged		
Motor Vehicles			Trash Service		
Courts			Ensures Fair Treatment		
Army, Navy, etc.			Patents		
Post Office			Help Other Nations		
Museums			Protects Borders		
Parks			Weather Service		
Protect the Environment			Dams and Bridges		
Protect Consumers					
Medical Research					
Aid for the Poor					

Decisions, Decisions

Springboard:
    Students should complete the
    "Who Should Decide?" survey.
(Answers will vary but should be explained and spark discussion.)

Objective: The student will be able to explain how decision-making occurs in the three main types of economies: market, command, and mixed.

Materials:
Who Should Decide? (Springboard handout)
Economics & Us (cut-out cards)
Pennies or token squares cut from construction paper (60 per group)
In the Real World (handout)

Terms to know:
citizen - member of a community, state, or nation

Procedure:

• After discussing student responses to the Springboard survey, explain that *decisions are made in different ways in different countries*. Go on to explain that *this lesson examines three different ways economic decisions are made.*

• **For group instruction** put students into groups of three and have them number off 1 through 3. Distribute the "Economics & Us" cards as follows: Give the 1's in each group "Market Economy" cards, all the 2's "Command Economy" cards, and the 3's the "Mixed Economy" cards. Allow a few minutes for them to study their instructions as you distribute 60 pennies or tokens per group. Then have the students complete their simulations.

• **For individualized instruction** work with the student to complete all three simulations, acting as the leader so you can make minor modifications as needed.

• Then hand out "In the Real World" and have the student(s) complete the analysis questions individually or in their groups.

• Have them share / compare their answers. The answer page provided should help guide discussion.

Who SHOULD Decide?

DIRECTIONS: Consider all these decisions that should be made and place an "X" in the column under who you think should make this decision.

DECISION	CITIZENS	GOVERNMENT	BOTH
How schools are run			
When roads are repaired			
How many soldiers we should send to war			
How many police officers are needed			
Where you can get medical care			
Who can go to school			
If there should be a park			
Who should pay for a new sewer line			
What should be a crime			

On the whole, when do you think it is better for the government to make decisions?

When is it better for the citizens to make those decisions?

What decisions should be made by both the people and the government? How?

MARKET ECONOMY

- You will go first in the simulation. You should place all the pennies in the middle of the table. Tell your group that when you say "go" they should grab as many pennies as they can.

- Then explain that in a market economy people can own businesses to make money. People can get rich or lose everything, and everything in between! A person who works hard earns money. A person who doesn't work gets nothing. People and businesses make their own decisions.

Discuss these questions in your group:
1. Who got the most pennies? Why was he/she able to do that?
2. In what ways was the simulation like the way a market economy works?
3. What do you think is good and bad about a market economy?

COMMAND ECONOMY

- You will go last in the simulation. You are the leader and will decide how many pennies each person gets. Explain that no one is allowed to question your decisions, and your decisions are final!

- Then explain that in a command economy the government or ruler decides who should do what. The government decides the goods and services to sell, who earns how much, and everything else.

Discuss these questions in your group:
1. Who got the most pennies? Why?
2. In what ways was the simulation like the way a command economy works?
3. What do you think is good and bad about a command economy?

MIXED ECONOMY

- You will go second in the simulation. First, tell your group the rules: No one can take more than 5 coins on a turn. However, a player can give up the 5 pennies to take any number from another player.

- Then explain that in a mixed economy the government makes rules that people and businesses must follow. But other than following those rules, people and businesses can make their own economic decisions. Some people can be very rich, and others may be poor.

Discuss these questions in your group:
1. Who got the most pennies? Why?
2. In what ways was the simulation like the way a mixed economy works?
3. What do you think is good and bad about a mixed economy?

In the Real World

1. Which type of economic system do you think our country has? Why?

   _____

   _____

   _____

   _____

2. Which system do you think is most fair? Why? _____

   _____

   _____

   _____

3. Which system do you think is the best? Why? _____

   _____

   _____

   _____

   _____

4. Which system do you think makes the best use of resources? Why? _____

   _____

   _____

   _____

   _____

5. Explain the pros and cons of each system:
   market - _____

   _____

   _____

   command - _____

   _____

   _____

   mixed - _____

   _____

   _____

1. Which type of economic system do you think our country has? Why?

   The U.S., Canada, most of Latin America, all of Europe, India, Japan, and most world nations have mixed economies. Their governments make laws and rules that people and businesses must obey. It also is involved in many other aspects of the economy, as shown in the last lesson (libraries, parks, etc.). However, people can choose their own jobs, own businesses, earn incomes, etc., but they must pay taxes to the government to pay for its services and costs of running the country.

2. Which system do you think is most fair? Why?

   Answers will vary but should be explained. In some command systems, the government ensures workers' pay is fairly equal. This can be done by controlling all the businesses and paying workers equally. It can also be achieved by making people who make more pay higher taxes, which are used to pay for many people's needs: health care, education, etc. A number of countries around the world actually do the latter. The downside is that people need not work as hard, since they'll end up with the same amount of money, have health care, education, etc. no matter what they do or don't do, which could impact production.

3. Which system do you think is best? Why?

   Answers will vary but should be explained. As noted, most countries in the world have a mixed economy, though the amount of government control can vary in these.

4. Which system do you think makes the best use of resources? Why?

   Answers will vary but should be explained. Command economies COULD but often have greedy leaders who care more about their own comfort and power than people or the environment. Mixed economies such as the U.S. have laws to protect the environment, which can be very helpful. Market economies might also make good use of resources if it works in the best interest of people and businesses.

5. Explain the pros and cons of each system:

   market - *People and businesses have a great deal of freedom. There is no limit to how much they can earn. On the other hard, people may work hard and still not make enough. There is no "safety net" for them or anyone else. Also, resources may be mismanaged or wasted if it serves the purposes of businesses.*

   command - *Everyone will usually get something whether they earn it or not, since resources may distributed equally. Of course, depending upon the person or people in charge, the citizens may also get nothing.*

   mixed - *The government makes laws and rules intended to make people and businesses treat consumers fairly. It may also make laws to protect the environment, workers, the community, etc. Still, there are those who may be quite poor and others who are EXTREMELY rich!*

Springboard:

Students should complete the "Import/Export Sort."*(Answers should make sense.)*

Objective: The student will be able to explain how trade makes countries interdependent with one another for goods and services.

Materials:
Import/Export Sort (Springboard handout)
Trading Cards (¼-page set per group, cut out)
ball of yarn (or string) per group
Our Interdependent World (handout)

Terms to know:
interdependence – when countries rely on each other to meet their needs and wants
embargo - not allowing trade

Procedure:

- During discussion of the Springboard, explain that *trading products, (importing and exporting), allows nations to have what they need and want*. Go on to explain that *this lesson examines the fourth sector of an economy, the foreign sector or trade with other nations*.

- Yet another simulation- this one on trade and interdependence. (Economics just lends itself to simulations. **For individualized instruction** arrange for a group situation.) Students, as the countries on the cards, should work in groups of five in a circle. Each should be given one of the "Trading Cards" and a minute to study their cards to decide which products they need to import and what they have to export.

- Give one student in each group the ball of yarn. He/she should announce one export product. The student who needs to import that item should call for it.

- The exporting student (country) should hold on to the end of the yarn and toss the ball to the importer. That student then announces an export, holds onto the string, and tosses the yarn ball to the student who wants to import it. Continue until all goods from the cards have been imported and exported.

- Then introduce the term "embargo" (*review term*) and explain that *due to a situation in that country, the other nations have placed an embargo on Colombia*. Have the students do the same activity again, omitting Colombia.

- Distribute "Our Interdependent World" and have the student(s) complete the analysis.

- Have them share their ideas and discuss. (*Possible answers include*:
  ○ *Some countries produce some goods and services, while others produce other things. Trade allows for all to have what they need or want.*
  ○ *For various reasons the world nations may agree to stop trading with a country, or impose an embargo.*
  ○ *Involvement in terrorism, mistreatment of citizens, ignoring global trade or other rules, etc. can result in embargoes.*
  ○ *It could have the intended result and the nation could change its ways. It can also impact others, causing shortages of goods that nations produce.*)

Import/Export Sort

DIRECTIONS: Imports and exports can be natural resources, farm products, or factory-made goods. Sort the products listed into the boxes where they fit. Then add as some examples of your own to each list.

cars	coffee	grain	computers
metal	oil	rice	clothing
bananas	airplanes	lumber	wheat
oranges	coal	furniture	cell phones
stoves	DVD's	water	TV's
video games	milk	tractors	minerals

Natural Resources	Farm Products	Factory Goods

Explain at least **2 REASONS** why countries would have imports and exports: _____

_____

_____

_____

_____

_____

TRADING CARDS

United States Imports: cars, coffee Exports: grain, computers	**United States** Imports: cars, coffee Exports: grain, computers
Colombia Imports: grain, cloth Exports: coffee, bananas	**Colombia** Imports: grain, cloth Exports: coffee, bananas
Great Britain Imports: computers, bananas Exports: metal, airplanes	**Great Britain** Imports: computers, bananas Exports: metal, airplanes
Japan Imports: metal, oil Exports: cars, rice	**Japan** Imports: metal, oil Exports: cars, rice
Saudi Arabia Imports: rice, airplanes Exports: oil, cloth	**Saudi Arabia** Imports: rice, airplanes Exports: oil, cloth
United States Imports: cars, coffee Exports: grain, computers	**United States** Imports: cars, coffee Exports: grain, computers
Colombia Imports: grain, cloth Exports: coffee, bananas	**Colombia** Imports: grain, cloth Exports: coffee, bananas
Great Britain Imports: computers, bananas Exports: metal, airplanes	**Great Britain** Imports: computers, bananas Exports: metal, airplanes
Japan Imports: metal, oil Exports: cars, rice	**Japan** Imports: metal, oil Exports: cars, rice
Saudi Arabia Imports: rice, airplanes Exports: oil, cloth	**Saudi Arabia** Imports: rice, airplanes Exports: oil, cloth

DIRECTIONS: Use what you learned in the lesson to explain your ideas about each point.

Explain how our world is interdependent. Include examples. _____

_____

_____

_____

_____

_____

_____

How does an embargo work? _____

_____

_____

_____

_____

_____

Why do you think nations might place an embargo on a country? _____

_____

_____

_____

_____

_____

What do you think are some opportunity costs of an embargo? _____

_____

_____

_____

_____

_____

_____

Go Global!

Springboard:
Students should analyze the "U.S. Clothing Imports" graph
and answer the questions.

Objective: The student will be able to explain trade balances in global economics.

Materials: U.S. Clothing Imports (Springboard handout)
         Balanced Trade? (2-page handout)
         Go Right to the Source (handout)

Terms to Know: **trade balance** - the difference between a countries imports and exports (or exports and imports)

Procedure:

- During discussion of the last Springboard question, explain that _we import clothing from these countries because they can produce them for less money, often because they pay workers so little. Even with the cost of transporting the goods to the U.S., the price is still lower than many U.S. products._

- Have the student(s) check inside their shirt labels, jackets, shoes, etc. to see where they were made. *(Many are likely imports.)* Have them name other imports. *(cars, computers, TV's, etc.)* Then discuss the following questions:
  - ? What problems can result if a country, in this case the U.S. has TOO MANY imports? *(Jobs are lost, and money that could have supported U.S. companies goes to companies or governments elsewhere.)*
  - ? What do you think would be the PERFECT import-export situation? *(If not suggested, explain that the IDEAL trade situation is to have about the same amount of imports as exports.)*

- Introduce the term "trade balance" and explain that _this lesson looks at the U.S. compared to its trading partners in terms of the value of goods traded_.

- Distribute the "Balanced Trade?" and "Go Right to the Source" handouts. The student(s) should work individually, in pairs, or small groups to analyze the graphs to complete the chart, identifying the sources that provide the answers and stating them. (Graphs based on information from the U.S. Census Bureau and Industry Canada.)

- Have them share their answers and discuss.

- **EXTENSION:** Challenge the student(s) to survey and tally 100 products to find out what number (percentage) of the 100 items are imports. Have them share/compare their results.

U.S. Clothing Imports

Latin America
Mainland China
East Asia
Western Europe
Southeast Asia
South Asia
Africa & Middle East
Russia
Eastern Europe

■ 1992-93
□ 2001-02

7.5   15.0   22.5   30.0

In BILLIONS of U.S. Dollars

Where do the **MOST** clothing imports come to the U.S. from?
- A. Latin America
- B. Mainland China
- C. Western Europe
- D. Eastern Europe

Which country most recently began exporting clothes to the United States?
- A. Latin America
- B. Western Europe
- C. South Asia
- D. Russia

Which statement is true based on the graph?
- A. U.S. clothing imports rose from 1993-2002.
- B. The U.S. exports more clothing than it imports.
- C. People in Eastern Europe hardly ever wear clothing.
- D. Mainland China produces more clothing than any nation.

Which number is nearest the **AVERAGE** value of U.S. clothing imports?
- A. 7.5 million
- B. 10 billion
- C. 15 million
- D. 22 billion

Which sentence states an opportunity cost of the U.S. of importing so much clothing?
- A. U.S. consumers have a wider range of choices in clothing.
- B. Clothing costs less since labor costs less in other countries.
- C. U.S. clothing companies don't need as many American workers.
- D. The government can charge import taxes on clothing brought in.

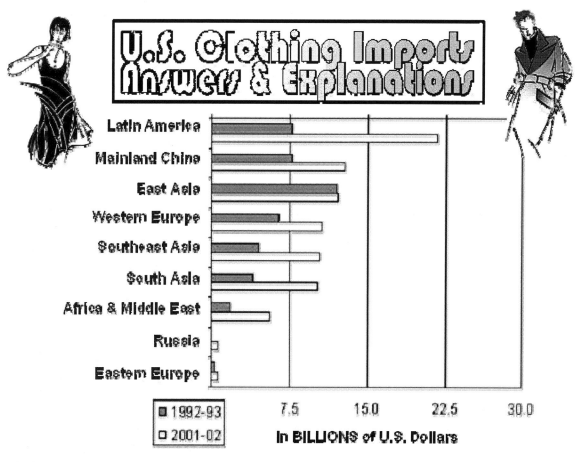

U.S. Clothing Imports Answers & Explanations

In BILLIONS of U.S. Dollars

- 1992-93
- 2001-02

Where do the **MOST** clothing imports come to the U.S. from?
- A. Latin America *
- B. Mainland China
- C. Western Europe
- D. Eastern Europe

(At least in 2001-02 Latin America seemed to lead the rest of the world in clothing exports to the U.S.)

Which country most recently began exporting clothes to the United States?
- A. Latin America
- B. Western Europe
- C. South Asia
- D. Russia *

(Russia is the only listing with no bar for 1992-93.)

Which statement is true based on the graph?
- A. U.S. clothing imports rose from 1993-2002. *
- B. The U.S. exports more clothing than it imports.
- C. People in Eastern Europe hardly ever wear clothing.
- D. Mainland China produces more clothing than any nation.

(B and D cannot be determined based on the graph, and Choice C is ridiculous.)

Which number is nearest the **AVERAGE** value of U.S. clothing imports?
- A. 7.5 million   B. 10 billion *   C. 15 million   D. 22 billion

(No calculation is necessary, and even if students don't know how to calculate "average," they can answer by eliminating "millions." D is the high end.)

Which sentence states an opportunity cost of the U.S. of importing so much clothing?
- A. U.S. consumers have a wider range of choices in clothing.
- B. Clothing costs less since labor costs less in other countries.
- C. U.S. clothing companies don't need as many American workers. *
- D. The government can charge import taxes on clothing brought in.

(Choices A, B, and D are all good for the U.S. C is what is given up.)

Total Value of U.S. Imports & Exports
In <u>BILLIONS</u> of U.S. Dollars

Source #1:

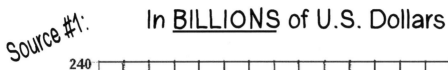

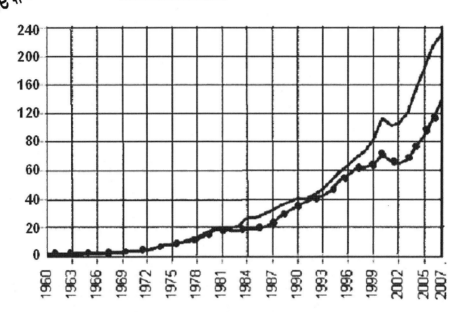

— **Total value of U.S. imports**

←• **Total value of U.S. exports**

Source #2:

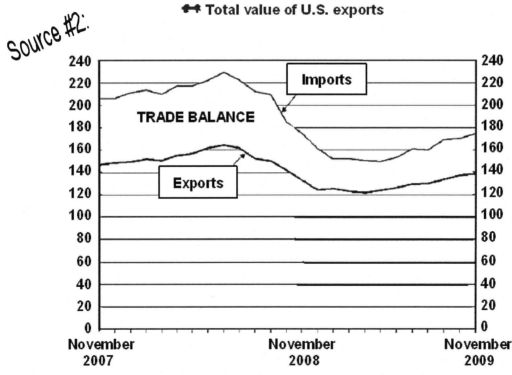

BALANCED TRADE?

America's Top Trading Partners
How Do They Stack Up?

Source #3:

RANK	COUNTRY	2009 TOTAL IMPORTS	2009 TOTAL EXPORTS
1	Canada	203.6	186.5
2	China	269.9	61.2
3	Mexico	159.5	117.2
4	Japan	86.4	46.2
5	Germany	64.3	39.3
6	United Kingdom	43.5	42.0
7	South Korea	35.8	25.8
8	France	31.1	24.3
9	Netherlands	14.8	29.7
10	Taiwan	25.7	16.4
11	Brazil	18.2	23.7
12	Italy	24.1	11.2
13	Singapore	14.3	20.1
14	India	19.4	15.0
15	Venezuela	25.3	8.7

Source #4: ## Canada's Imports from & Exports to the U.S.

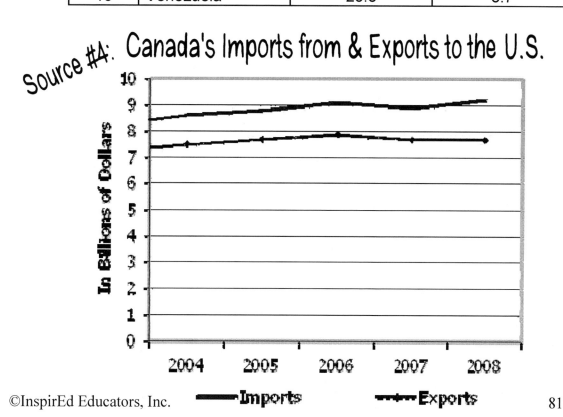

Go Right to the Source

QUESTION	SOURCE(S)	ANSWER
Which country is America's biggest trading partner?		
Describe the U.S.'s trade balance.		
Which country or countries export more than they import?		
Describe Canada's total trade balance.		
Has the U.S. ever had an equal balance of imports and exports? If so, when?		
Which country has the biggest difference between imports and exports?		
What happened to U.S. trade in 2008 and 2009?		
Describe Canada's trade with the U.S.		
Which country do you think has the BEST trade balance? Why?		
Overall, what trend do you see in U.S. trade over the years?		

Go Right to the Source – Suggested Answers and Explanations

QUESTION	SOURCE(S)	ANSWER
Which country is America's biggest trading partner?	Source 3	Canada, since the two large nations share a very long border.
Describe the U.S.'s trade balance.	Sources 1 and 2	On the whole the U.S. imports more than it exports.
Which country or countries export more than they import?	Source 3	Of the U.S.'s top 15 trading partners, only the Netherlands, Brazil, and Singapore export more than they import.
Describe Canada's total trade balance.	Source 3	In 2009 it imported more than it exported.
Has the U.S. ever had an equal balance of imports and exports? If so, when?	Source 1	From about 1960 to 1981 the U.S. had an equal balance of trade.
Which country has the biggest difference between imports and exports?	Source 3	At least in 2009, China had the largest difference.
What happened to U.S. trade in 2008 and 2009?	Source 2	Trade declined due to poor economic conditions in the nation and the world.
Describe Canada's trade with the U.S.	Source 4	Canada imports more goods/services from the U.S. than it exports.
Which country do you think has the BEST trade balance? Why?	Source 3	Answers may vary, but the U.K. showed almost a perfect trade balance in 2009.
Overall, what trend do you see in U.S. trade over the years?	Source 1	Except for the decline in 2008-9, U.S. trade has steadily increased.

Springboard:
Students should read the "What's It Made Of? information
and complete the chart. *(Charts will vary.)*

Objective: The student will be able to explain how economic and environmental concerns can clash.

Materials:	What's It Made Of? (Springboard handout) A Town Divided (handout) More Facts of the Matter (2 sets of cut-out cards)
Terms to know:	**synthetic** - man-made from chemicals to be like the real thing **environment** - the world around us **debate** - two views on a subject; argue the two views

Procedure:

• During discussion of the Springboard, have the student(s) look around and find other things besides clothing made of natural and synthetic materials. *(Wooden furniture, metal shelves, Formica tables, etc.)* Explain that *many people in the nation and the world are beginning to use more natural products and in general be more "green," (aware of their impact on the environment). Of course there are also many people who disagree and think a strong economy is more important than the environment.* Go on to explain that *this lesson looks at one example of the push-pull between economics and the environment.*

• Distribute "A Town Divided." Read together or have the student(s) read the background information and complete the handout.

• Then explain that *the student(s) will now pretend to be the townspeople of Little Oak. Today the town is having a meeting to discuss the possible sale of the forest.* Then clear your throat, look official, and announce:

   Ladies and Gentlemen, as mayor of Little Oak I want to welcome you to this town meeting. As you know, we have a decision to make: whether or not to sell our forest for a housing development. There are many good arguments for both sides, and we want to give all who came today a chance to share their ideas.
   To keep the discussion kind and organized, I thought we could hold a debate. Why don't all those in favor of the land sale go over there (point to a gathering place) *and those against it there* (point to another gathering place)? *Now, both groups should take a few minutes to get organized and plan their arguments.*

• **For group instruction** allow about 5-10 minutes for discussion. During that time, randomly hand each side one set of "More Facts of the Matter" cards, one card at a time. Hand the cards to a "leader," a student you think can command the attention of the group and keep order. (The cards introduce points for both sides of the argument to help stimulate ideas and discussion.) **For individualized instruction** read the cards together, have the student select which side to argue, and allow time to organize his/her arguments. Then debate with the student, arguing the viewpoint he/she did not choose.

- Then (again, as the mayor) explain that *to ensure that our debate is orderly, we will abide by some simple rules*:
    1. *First, we must decide which of the two sides will open the debate.* (Do this; a coin toss or picking a number from 1-10, which you've written down would be fair.)
    2. (Then continue) *To begin, one member of the side going first introduces a point.*
    3. *One member from the other side will be called on to argue against that point.*
    4. *Then one member from each side may debate the point.*
    5. *Then the other side offers a new point, which may be commented upon three times before another argument is offered.*
    6. *Arguments should be made in an orderly rotation between the two sides of the debate.*
    7. *No one should speak or yell out unless called upon.*

- Once the debate has ended, lead a follow-up discussion of these questions:
    ? How does the situation in Little Oak provide an example of the push-pull between the economy and caring for the environment? *(The town's economy needed help, and a large building project offered it. But the project would harm the environment and destroy the only green space.)*
    ? Can you think of other examples in which the economy and environment clash? *(Answers may vary and include: offshore oil drilling, logging in national parks, funding for parks and environmental projects, etc.)*

- **EXTENSION:** Have the student(s) watch the news, talk to family members, read stories online or in the newspaper, etc. to find a current example of the clash between environmental concerns and the economy. Then have them share what they learn.

What's It Made Of?

Clothes can be made of many things. Some are natural; they come from plants or animals. Other clothes are made of synthetic, or man-made, materials.

Natural materials in clothes include: cotton, wool, silk, down, and others. Polyester is a man-made synthetic that can be made to look like natural ones.

Can you tell the difference? Does it matter? Look at your clothes and see what you think.

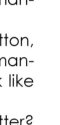

DIRECTIONS: Look at the labels in yours and some friends' clothes to see what they are made of. **(But be POLITE!)** Then list each item where it fits in the chart and tell what the material **IS** or what it **LOOKS LIKE**:

Natural Materials	Synthetic Materials

NOW: Why do you think companies would make fabrics that **LOOK LIKE** they're natural, but they're not? _____

_____

_____

_____

_____

A Town Divided

The town of Little Oaks is divided. They cannot agree on what to do with a large forest in their community. It is a lovely place, filled with plants and animals. Many people spend time there. They hike, picnic, and jog. In fact the forest is really the only big green space in town. Also water from the forest drains into a nearby river. And many people like to swim and fish in that river.

Now there is a big builder in town who wants to buy the forest. He wants to clear the land and build 200 homes. The houses will be in a good price range. This is important because many of the homes in Little Oaks cost too much for most people to afford. The town owns the land and must decide whether or not to sell the forest to the builder.

The sale of the land would bring needed money to the town. The local elementary school needs repairs and many roads need fixing. The money would be put to good use! Also, many in town would like to buy one of the new houses. And building the houses would bring many new jobs.

Once the new homes are built, there will be more people in town paying taxes. The houses might even attract more people to Little Oaks. That would mean more business for local stores. Selling the forest has the town divided. The town citizens are going to vote to decide what to do.

Explain the two views of the forest debate:

1. _____

_____

_____

_____

_____

_____

2. _____

_____

_____

_____

_____

_____

More Facts of the Matter

About 3/4 of the people in town use the forest and nearby river. Many hike, hunt, picnic, swim, and fish. There is even a small area for camping.	The builder who wants to buy the land has lived in Little Oaks all his life. He is well-liked and has always "given back" to the town when he could.
Business in Little Oaks has been in a slump for a while. More people working and moving to town would REALLY help!	The forest is home to more than 30 different kinds of animals.
There is a great need in Little Oaks for affordable homes. The only things built in the past ten years have been apartments.	The town government has also been hurt by the economic slump. It needs money badly!
Once the forest is gone, the animals will either die or move. They could even, as in other places, move into people's yards and pose a danger.	The forest keeps the water that drains into the river clean. Runoff from clearing the land could harm the river.
More people in town could pose problems. Schools will be too crowded, and services such as the police and fire departments may not be as good.	Building 200 homes would provide jobs for many in the area. Local businesses will also be helped as people buy things for their new homes.
All the new houses will hurt the town's water supply. Run-off with fertilizer from lawns will harm the river and maybe the town's drinking water, too.	About one out of ten people in Little Oaks does not have a job now. Others are working for low pay just to have some money coming in.
More housing will bring more people and businesses to town. Little Oaks needs to perk up before people start leaving for better places to live!	More people living in town will mean more tax dollars. The extra money would help the community in many ways!

Hitting the Books

Springboard:

Students should complete the "I Read…" handout
as a guide for writing a short book review.

Objective: The student will be able to identify examples of economics concepts they have learned in books they read.

Materials: I Read… (Springboard handout)
Find an Example (handout)

Procedure:

- After allowing time for the student(s) to share their thoughts on the book(s) read, explain that _the student(s) will apply information and situations from their book(s) to what they have learned about economics in this unit_.
- Distribute the "Find an Example" handout. Have the student(s) work individually or in small groups to discuss and complete the handout. **NOTE:** Student(s) may not be able to find examples of everything in their books. For group instruction, you may wish to have students pair up and share examples if they read different books.
- Have them share their examples and discuss.

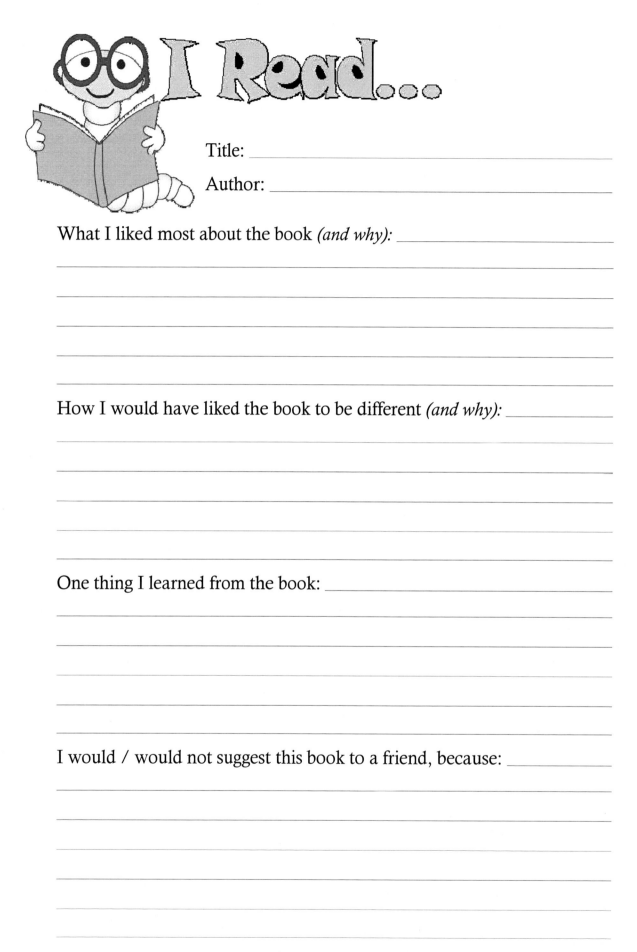

I Read...

Title: _____

Author: _____

What I liked most about the book *(and why):* _____

_____

_____

_____

_____

_____

How I would have liked the book to be different *(and why):* _____

_____

_____

_____

_____

_____

One thing I learned from the book: _____

_____

_____

_____

_____

I would / would not suggest this book to a friend, because: _____

_____

_____

_____

_____

_____

_____

FIND AN EXAMPLE

DIRECTIONS: Find an example of each economic term or idea in the book(s) you read. Jot notes to briefly explain each.

scarcity of resources:

goods or services:

imports / exports:

saving:

opportunity cost:

budgets:

entrepreneur:

competition:

supply and demand:

currency / money:

production:

specialization:

technology:

interdependence:

Reviewing Term$

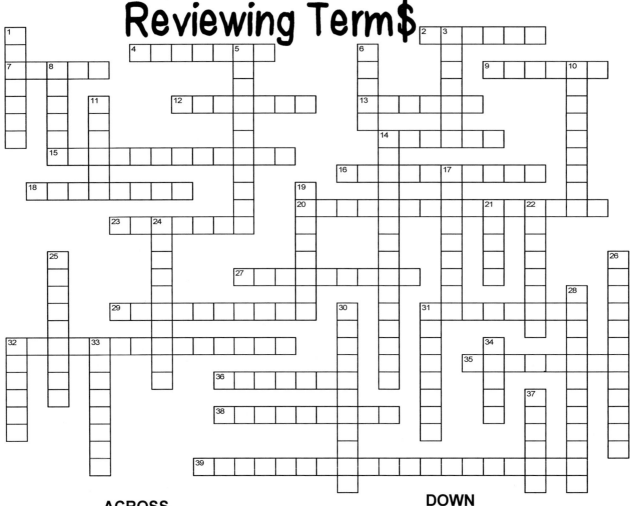

ACROSS

2 level of need or want for a product
4 member of a community, state, etc.
7 workers
9 deal back and forth to trade
12 money, buildings, machines, etc.
13 send goods to other countries for sale
14 good brought in
15 difference between imports and exports
16 money taken out of a bank
18 money earned from bank deposits
20 what is given up when a decision is made
23 money put into a bank
27 used to meet needs and wants
29 new ways to make work faster
31 work done for someone
32 doing one task well
35 one who buys goods and services
36 cost of goods or services
38 make products and businesses known
39 all that is needed to provide goods and services

DOWN

1 amount of money in an account
3 forbid trade
5 the world around us
6 bills and coins
8 plan for spending
10 use of resources to meet needs and wants
11 different views on a subject
14 relying on each other
17 not likely to be used up
19 when there is no competition
21 money paid to the government
22 used to pay for things
24 making goods
25 man-made to be like a real thing
26 one who opens and runs a business
28 workers each do one small part of production
30 businesses offering the same goods or services
31 not enough of something
32 amount of a good or service available
33 all of the businesses offering a good or service
34 things that are bought and sold
37 money made from business

Reviewing Term$ Puzzle Anwer

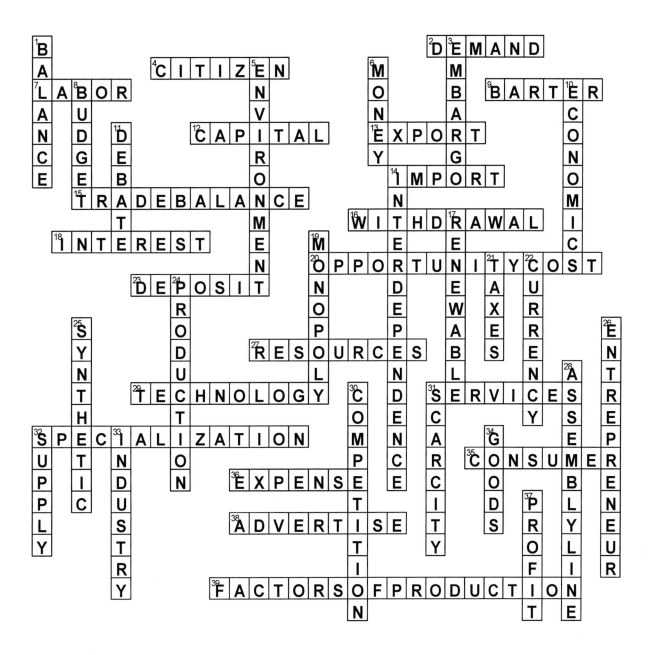

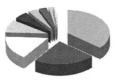

Economic$ & Me (A)

Matching – Write the letter of the correct answer in the blank:

_____ 1. renewable
_____ 2. consumer
_____ 3. import
_____ 4. budget
_____ 5. entrepreneur
_____ 6. barter
_____ 7. currency
_____ 8. monopoly
_____ 9. specialization
_____ 10. embargo

A. product bought from another country
B. dealing back and forth to make a trade
C. doing just one task well
D. a business that has no competition
E. plan for spending money
F. someone who buys goods and services
G. not allowing trade
H. one who starts and runs a business
I. anything used to pay for goods and services
J. not likely to run out

Give one example of each of these terms:

11. resource - _____

12. good - _____

13. labor - _____

14. industry - _____

15. money - _____

Multiple Choice - Write the letter of the correct answer in the blank:

_____ 16. Which of these economic sectors deals with imports and exports?
    A. household   B. government   C. business   D. foreign

_____ 17. Which of these is **NOT** a factor of production?
    A. resources   B. competition   C. labor   D. capital

_____ 18. In general if demand is ___, the price will ____.
    A. low … be high   C. low … increase
    B. high … decrease   D. high … be high

_____ 19. Which sentence is true about mass production?
    A. Factories often have assembly lines.
    B. No factors of production are involved in it.
    C. All mass-produced goods are exported.
    D. Mass produced products are made by hand.

Fully answer the following question:
20. Explain how market, command, and mixed economies differ.

The first American bank was in Philadelphia. It and other early banks were not the safest places for money. Banks had no rules, and many people lost their deposits. This was a huge problem during the Great Depression of the 1930's. When the economy crashed, people panicked and tried to withdraw their money. The banks did not have enough cash to give people, since they loan money to people to buy homes and start businesses. Since they didn't have enough money, thousands of banks closed. Many, many people lost all their savings.

Afterwards, laws were passed to make banks safer. The most important **reform** was to form the Federal Deposit Insurance Corporation, or FDIC. The FDIC, run by the government, protects bank deposits. If a bank closes, the government will cover up to $250,000 of the money people have in that bank. The FDIC oversees banks to make sure they follow banking rules. It can also loan money and even take over banks in danger of closing.

_____ 21. The word "reform" in the reading **MOST NEARLY** means
   A. improvement.　　B. bank.　　C. decline.　　D. weakness.

_____ 22. A good title for this passage would be
   A. "A Long History of Banking."
   B. "Making Banks Better and Safer."
   C. "Bank On Losing Your Money."
   D. "FDIC and The Great Depression"

_____ 23. Which of these statements is **TRUE** based on the reading?
   A. Everyone trusted banks until the Great Depression.
   B. The first banks were safe for everyone's money.
   C. No banks have closed since the FDIC formed.
   D. The FDIC solved many banking problems.

Expense	Budgeted	Actual	Difference
Rent	$500	$500	$0
Phone	$50	$60	+$10
Food	$150	$125	-$25
Electric	$75	$75	$0
Entertainment	$40	$50	+10

_____ 24. The chart above would **BEST** be described as a/an
   A. electric deposit.　　　　C. monthly budget.
   B. savings account.　　　　D. check withdrawal.

_____ 25. Which of these statements shows an opportunity cost in the chart?
   A. Rent for this person went up this month from last month.
   B. A cold snap caused a spike in this month's heating bills.
   C. This person spent less on food in order to go to a movie.
   D. Overall, spending this month was what was expected.

Economic$ & Me (B)

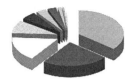

Fill in the blanks with unit terms:

1. The only electric company in the state holds a/an _____.

2. _____ buy the goods and services in an economy.

3. The _____ took a risk to open and run her own business.

4. The government pays for services with money from _____.

5. Items sent to be sold in other countries are called _____.

6. The_____ kept nations from trading with North Korea.

7. The _____ is how people meet their needs for goods and services.

8. _____ allows workers to each do one task very well.

9. Money is the most popular form of _____ used.

10. Business _____ includes money, machines, and buildings.

Give one example of each of these terms:

11. import - _____

12. service - _____

13. citizen - _____

14. industry - _____

15. renewable resource - _____

Multiple Choice – Write the letter of the correct answer in the blank:

_____ 16. Which statement about the four sectors of an economy is **FALSE**?
   A. The household sector decides what things cost.
   B. The business sector sells goods and services.
   C. The government sector makes laws and rules.
   D. The foreign sector involves imports and exports.

_____ 17. Which of these factors is **LEAST** important to production?
   A. resources   C. capital
   B. labor   D. advertising

_____ 18. Decisions in a command economy are usually made by
   A. citizens.   C. entrepreneurs.
   B. banks.   D. the government

_____ 19. In general if supply is low, demand will be ____ and price will be ____.
   A. low … high   C. low … low
   B. high … high   D. high … low

Fully answer the following question on your own paper and attach:

20. Why do you think most companies make goods using mass production?

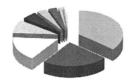

Economic$ & Me (C)

Fill in the blanks with unit terms:

1. Surplus is to too much, as _____ is to not enough.
2. Pay is to a worker, as _____ is to a business.
3. Income is to money one gets, as _____ is to money spent.
4. Car is to vehicle, as money is to _____.
5. A penalty is to sports, as a/an _____ is to trade.
6. Bills are to companies, as _____ are to the government.
7. A diet is to eating, as a/an _____ is to spending money.
8. Part is to whole, as worker is to _____.
9. Real life is to make-believe, as natural products are to _____.
10. A consequence is to a life decision, as _____ is to an economic choice.

Give one example of each of these terms:

11. factor of production - _____
12. debate - _____
13. service - _____
14. scarce resource - _____
15. renewable resource - _____

Multiple Choice - Write the letter of the correct answer in the blank:

_____ 16. Which of these is the **BEST** example of technology?
   A. The boss hires a new factory worker.
   B. A new company president was named.
   C. Another holiday was added to the calendar.
   D. The company's equipment has been updated.

_____ 17. Receive is to ___, as give is to ___.
   A. labor … capital   C. supply … demand
   B. profit … expense   D. export … import

_____ 18. Decisions in a command economy are usually made by
   A. the government   C. citizens.
   B. entrepreneurs.   D. banks.

_____ 19. Which statement is **TRUE** based on the laws of supply and demand?
   A. A popular toy sells out and its price drops dramatically.
   B. Three shoe stores on one block mean higher prices for all.
   C. A fancy new phone drives prices of the old version way up.
   D. Flower prices soar during the week before Valentine's Day.

Fully answer the following question on your own paper and attach:

20. Why do you think the assembly line has become the norm for production?

Form A:

1. J
2. F
3. A
4. E
5. H
6. B
7. I
8. D
9. C
10. G

11. wood, minerals, people, etc.
12. car, clothing, TV, toy, etc.
13. factory worker, dentist, sales clerk, etc.
14. computers, automobiles, construction, etc
15. dollars, cents, pesos, euros, etc.
16. D
17. B
18. D
19. A
20. Answers will vary but the main difference is who makes economic decisions: people and businesses in a market economy; the government in a command economy; both in a mixed economy.

Form B:

1. monopoly
2. Consumers
3. entrepreneur
4. taxes
5. exports
6. embargo
7. economy
8. Specialization
9. currency
10. capital

11. cars, cameras, computers, etc. *(Brand names are fine.)*
12. cleaners, mechanic, doctor, etc.
13. almost anyone, teacher, parents, etc.
14. computers, automobiles, construction, etc
15. water, soil, wind, sun, etc.
16. A
17. D
18. D
19. B
20. Goods can be made faster and cheaper, so more can be made available to consumers, often at lower prices.

Form C:

1. scarcity
2. profit
3. expense
4. currency
5. embargo
6. taxes
7. budget
8. assembly line
9. synthetic(s)
10. opportunity cost

11. resources, labor, capital
12. economy v. environment or any issue
13. teaching, dry cleaning, sales, accounting, etc.
14. gold, diamonds, oil, etc.
15. water, soil, wind, sun, etc.
16. D
17. B
18. A
19. D
20. Goods can be made faster and cheaper, so more can be made available to consumers, often at lower prices.

Skills Forms A-C:

21. A
22. B
23. D
24. C
25. C

RESOURCES

www.councilforeconed.org/ - Council for Economic Education Homepage, 2010.

ecedweb.unomaha.edu/home.cfm - Economic Education Web, 2009

www.jumpstartcoalition.org/ - Jump Start Coalition for Personal Financial Literacy, 2010.

www.heldref.org/pubs/jece/about.html - Journal of Economic Education, Heldref Publications, 2009.

www.frbsf.org/education/activities/drecon/askecon.cfm - "Ask Dr. Econ," Federal Reserve Bank of San Francisco, 2010.

www.frbsf.org/federalreserve/money/funfacts.html - "Fun Facts About Money," Federal Reserve Bank of San Francisco, 2010.

www.usa.gov/Agencies/Federal/All_Agencies/index.shtml - "A to Z Index of Government Departments and Agencies," USA.gov, Office of Citizen Services and Communication, 2010.

www.socialstudiesforkids.com/subjects/economics.htm - Economics, Social Studies for Kids, 2009.

www.kidsbank.com – "Sovereign Bank Presents," Kidsbank.com, 2009.

www.census.gov/indicator/www/ustrade.html - "Foreign Trade Statistics," U.S. Census Bureau, 2010.

www.usmint.gov/index.cfm?flash=yes - The U.S. Mint Official website, 2009.

www.fte.org/ - Foundation for Teaching Economics, 2010.

www.ic.gc.ca/eic/site/tdo-dcd.nsf/eng/home - "Trade Data Online," Industry Canada, 2009.

www.philadelphiafed.org/publications/economic-education/ - Economic Education: Publications and Other Resources, Federal Reserve Bank of Philadelphia, 2010.

www.kidsturncentral.com/links/moneylinks.htm - "Money - Resources for Kids," 2010.

www.moneyinstructor.com/lesson/opportunitycost.asp - "Opportunity Cost," Moneyinstructor.com, 2010.

I Think: Thematic Units

Some of our other **I Think** offerings include:

Series	Titles
I Think: Connections	Civilization, Democracy, Dictators, Ethnic Conflict, Indigenous People, Imperialism
I Think: U.S. History	Colonial America, American Revolution, Westward Expansion, The Civil War, Reconstruction Era, Problems & Progressives, The Modern Era, The African American Experience
I Think: Government	Electing the President, Civic Participation. The Constitution, The Executive, Legislative, and Judicial Branches
I Think: Geography	What Is Geography? World Geography by Region
I Think: World History	A wide variety of Ancient Civilizations units, Middle Ages, Renaissance, the World Wars, The Holocaust, etc.
I Think: Economics	What Is Economics? Personal Finance
I Think: Reading & Writing	Poetry, Short Stories, Literary Themes, Novels, Biographies, etc.
I Think: I Can!	Early Childhood Thematic units
I Think: It's Elementary!	America's Colonies, Revolution, Economics, U.S. Regions, etc.

We're adding more titles all the time.
Check our websites for current listings!

www.inspirededucators.com